AI EMPOWERED

The Psychology of Extraordinary Human-AI Collaboration

Aaron Douglas

Published by Auspicious LLC auspicious.llc

ISBN 979-8-9966324-0-4 (paperback)

First Edition, 2026

Printed in the United States of America

* * *

A note on AI in the making of this book

This book argues that the future of knowledge work depends on how humans collaborate with artificial intelligence. It would be dishonest to make that argument without practicing it. AI tools were used throughout the research, drafting, and production of this book as collaborative partners, not as substitutes for the thinking, judgment, and experience behind the ideas. Every claim was verified against primary sources. Every argument reflects the author's positions, developed over twenty years of working with people and their tools. The AI contributed scale and speed. The human contributed everything that made the scale worth having. That distinction is the thesis of this book.

The interactive companion to this book is free at airaa.org/empowered.

Dedicated to Amy Jo.

Contents

INTRODUCTION

The Pattern

Twelve-person marketing agency. The kind of shop where everybody knows every client by first name, where the account managers carry the relationships in their heads and pride themselves on never needing to look anything up. The founder has spent forty thousand dollars on a CRM that was supposed to change that: centralize the client history, track the conversations, make the institutional knowledge visible so the business wouldn't collapse if someone quit on a Friday.

Six months in, nobody has logged a single call.

Ask the founder why and he has reasons. The software is clunky. The interface isn't intuitive. The team doesn't have time to enter data when they're busy doing the actual work of serving clients. The reasons aren't wrong, exactly. But they're not the reason.

Here's the thing about tools that require transparency: they don't just change how you work. They change what you're willing to see about how you work. This CRM didn't ask the team to learn new software. It asked them to admit they didn't remember what they'd promised prospects last month. It asked them to make visible the gaps between what they said they did and what they actually did. That is why nobody opened it.

The tool worked. The humans couldn't use it without confronting something about themselves.

*

Different city, same pattern. A business owner hires an agency to redo his website. Good agency. They do the research, build the strategy, write copy grounded in what his customers actually search for. He approves every recommendation in the kickoff deck. Then, during review, he rewrites every headline.

He edits every page back to something worse. He couldn't tell you why. Ask, and he'll say something about "knowing my customers" and "trusting my gut." He isn't lying. He believes it. What's actually happening is a man protecting a story about himself that matters more than the outcome he's paying for. He rewrote the headlines because accepting them meant accepting that his expertise wasn't the differentiator he'd built his identity around.

Two businesses. Two different tools. Same failure. Both understood what the tool could do. Both invested real money and real time. The failure lived deeper than knowledge or commitment: in who they believed they were, and what accepting help from the tool would say about that belief.

*

If those two stories were only about a CRM and a website, they wouldn't be worth a book. They're worth a book because the same failure is now sitting at your desk.

Whatever you do for a living — medicine, law, engineering, marketing, education, finance — you've been handed a tool that can do parts of your job. And since November 2022, when ChatGPT launched, the pattern from those small conference rooms has been playing out everywhere, at a scale nobody could have imagined. Knowledge workers across every profession, every industry, every country have split into the same two camps.

Mode one: surrender. Paste in the request, accept whatever comes back, add nothing of your own. The consultant who types "create a Q4 marketing strategy" and sends the output to her client without a single insight she wouldn't have gotten from any other consultant with the same subscription. The content team that publishes seventy-seven AI-written financial articles and has to correct more than half, because nobody with actual expertise reviewed the math. The surrenderer feels efficient: look how much I got done today. The thinking got delegated along with the work. The tool runs. Nobody's steering.

Mode two: fight. Question every output, override every recommendation, wrap the resistance in the language of quality standards and professional rigor. The senior partner who'll let AI handle document review but won't allow it near case strategy. The faculty member who opts out because the tool can now do the things she'd built her professional identity around doing. The fighter feels rigorous. They've been handed help they refuse to be helped by. The tool sits there. Nobody's using it.

Both modes waste the tool's potential. Both feel rational from the inside. And both produce the same outcome: the human capability and the tool capability never actually combine.

In between the two camps, a smaller group is doing something different. They bring their expertise into the collaboration. They push back when the AI is wrong and accept when it's right. They treat the tool as something that amplifies their judgment rather than replacing it or insulting it. They're getting results nobody else is getting. Same tools. Same subscriptions. Different relationship.

This book is about what separates that group from everyone else. The answer isn't what most people think it is, and it isn't what most organizations are spending money on.

*

The pattern didn't start with ChatGPT. I'd watched it for twenty years before it had a name: running a marketing agency, sitting across conference tables from clients and the tools they'd bought and wouldn't use. My training is in psychology — before marketing, before any of it — and that wiring is why the pattern wouldn't leave me alone. In therapy, a client who says they can't sleep isn't asking for sleep hygiene. You ask what's keeping them awake. In a conference room, a client who says the CRM is too complicated isn't asking for a simpler CRM. You ask what using it would require them to admit. Same move. Different room. Half consultant, half something there isn't a clean word for. Organizational therapist is the closest I've found.

The founder in the first story was my client. So was the man who rewrote the headlines. And my best clients, maybe one in five, were the ones who did neither surrender nor fight. They brought their own judgment into the collaboration and let the tool do what it was good at. I couldn't teach the other four to be like them, and it wasn't for lack of trying. The gap between the two groups ran deeper than knowledge or skill: into how they saw themselves, and what they believed using the tool said about them.

The question that kept nagging at me: what are people protecting by not using their tools?

I didn't have an answer. Not a complete one. But I had a pattern, and it was consistent enough that I stopped thinking of it as individual client quirks and started thinking of it as something structural. Something about how humans relate to tools that do parts of their job. Then ChatGPT arrived, and the one-in-five showed up at global scale too: the same rare relationship, now visible in every profession at once. The gap between "a client doesn't use their CRM" and "humanity has access to the most powerful collaboration tool ever created and most people are wasting it" closed in about ninety days.

*

I wasn't the first person to see the pattern. I need to be honest about that.

Parasuraman and Riley described it in 1997, studying pilots and industrial automation operators. They gave the two modes clinical names: "misuse" for overreliance and "disuse" for underreliance, and documented how both degraded human-machine performance. Lisanne Bainbridge, even earlier, in 1983, described what she called the "ironies of automation": the more reliable you make the automated system, the more the human skills it needs as backup atrophy. The pattern was in the literature decades before I noticed it in a conference room.

What that work left open was the question underneath it. Parasuraman documented that people misuse and disuse their tools; he didn't say why any particular person, on any particular Tuesday, lands on one side or the other. The adoption research that came later, the models that predict whether someone will pick a tool up at all, stops at the door: it answers *will you use it*, and the CRM founder's problem started after yes. This book takes up the part those frameworks set down. Once you are using the tool, how much of you enters? And what decides that?

What kept surfacing, the thing the existing frameworks didn't quite reach, was identity. Knowledge, skill, and attitude were all present in the rooms where the tools went unused. The CRM founder understood his software perfectly. His resistance came from a different place: using it properly would have exposed something about how he ran his agency that didn't match the story he told himself. The business owner's headlines weren't the problem. Accepting them was. Because accepting them meant accepting that his expertise wasn't the differentiator he'd built his identity around, and that was a trade his sense of self wouldn't make.

The pattern is psychological. It's about who you believe you are in relation to the tool, and what using the tool well would require you to see about yourself. Identity and self-efficacy, this book will argue, often decide whether a person lands on misuse or disuse. Not always. Often enough to be the thing worth looking at first.

*

The research confirmed it was bigger than one consulting practice. And the data, which the next chapter lays out in full, is worse than you'd expect.

A 2024 meta-analysis of 106 experimental studies found that human-AI teams, on average, performed worse than the best of either humans or AI working alone. Measurably, consistently worse. The split tracked task type: on decision tasks, the combinations lost ground; on creation work, where the human brought domain expertise the AI couldn't generate, they gained. And the combinations that won were the ones where the human alone outperformed the AI alone. Value showed up when there was real human capability to bring, and it showed up nowhere else. Meanwhile, in an early-2025 experiment, experienced developers were 19 percent slower with AI tools and estimated they were 20 percent faster. The researchers have since said the slowdown itself is a snapshot of tools that have already changed; what didn't change is that the developers couldn't tell. In one study, higher AI literacy correlated with worse judgment of one's own AI-assisted work. Corporate America has poured billions into teaching people about the tools, and what that spending reliably produces is usage. Usage is not collaboration. In the studies that look past it, more knowledge shows up as more confident misuse.

Training should close the gap. Better tools should close it. Neither has. The tools keep getting more capable; the space between what they can do and what people actually get from them keeps growing. The problem lives in the relationship between the human and the tool. It always has.

*

That's what this book is about: what happens in the space between a capable human and a capable AI system, and why that space is almost always wasted.

The two failure modes aren't character flaws. They're predictable responses to a specific kind of psychological threat: a threat to professional identity, to the story you tell yourself about how you create value. And because the mechanism is psychological, the fix is too. This book gives you a model for seeing the space between you and the tool, and four conditions that separate the people who get extraordinary results from AI from the people who get almost nothing.

A word about what kind of model it is, because the word "model" promises different things to different readers. This one belongs to the family that includes Maslow's hierarchy, Vroom's expectancy theory, and Dweck's mindsets: frameworks for seeing, not instruments for calculating. It has the shape of an equation, and Chapter 4 explains why the shape matters. But you cannot measure its parts independently and multiply them, and nothing in this book will pretend otherwise. What the model does is make a mechanism visible that is otherwise invisible: the variable that sits between what you know and what the tool can do, and decides how much of each reaches the other. Once you can see that variable, you can see it move.

Four psychological shifts move it: recognizing yourself as the scarce input, understanding that the collaboration should demand more of you rather than less, seeing AI as something that clarifies your professional identity rather than threatening it, and building an ongoing calibration practice, because the judgment of when AI helps and when it hurts never runs on autopilot. They aren't steps or tips or the kind of thing you pick up from a training video, which is probably why almost nobody watches the video. They're shifts in how you understand your own role. That they reinforce one another is a working hypothesis, offered as one; the book will say where the evidence touches two of them at once and where it doesn't yet. What the four explain, together, is why one person with the same tool, the same training, and the same expertise produces work no one else could replicate, while the person at the next desk produces work that anyone with a subscription could have generated.

If that sounds like psychology rather than technology: good. It is. A research team in *Trends in Cognitive Sciences* published a framework arguing that generative AI threatens workers' basic psychological needs: competence, autonomy, relatedness. When a tool can do the work you've spent a career learning to do, it doesn't just change your workflow. It changes what you believe about your own value. The coping strategies the researchers identified were dissociation, escapism, and symbolic self-completion: clinical names for what plays out over conference room tables every day. Different rooms, different vocabulary, the same insight: the challenge is human.

The founder who spent forty thousand dollars on a CRM he couldn't use had a seeing problem. The tool required him to see something about his team that he wasn't ready to see, and rather than confront it, he blamed the software.

I think about him when I look at the AI adoption data. Billions of dollars invested. Usage climbing every quarter. Impact stubbornly flat. Organizations everywhere reporting the same thing: our people are using AI, but the work isn't getting better. They're looking for the fix in the technology: a better model, a better interface, a better training program. They're looking everywhere except at the space between the human and the tool. The space where the relationship lives. The space where almost everything is lost.

This book looks there. At the psychology underneath the productivity problem. At the identity dynamics underneath the adoption problem. At the four conditions that determine whether a human and an AI system produce something neither could produce alone, or produce nothing worth producing at all.

The question this book answers: what does it take to see clearly enough to use the tool well? And why is that question the one that will determine whether AI makes us better or just makes us busier?

Notes

1. CNET AI-generated financial articles, 2023. 77 articles published; more than half required corrections. Multiple news sources.
2. Parasuraman, R. & Riley, V. (1997). "Humans and automation: Use, misuse, disuse, abuse." *Human Factors*, 39(2), 230-253.

3. Bainbridge, L. (1983). "Ironies of automation." *Automatica*, 19(6), 775-779.

4. Vaccaro, M., Almaatouq, A., & Malone, T. (2024). "When combinations of humans and AI are useful: A systematic review and meta-analysis." *Nature Human Behaviour*, 8(12), 2293-2303. DOI: 10.1038/s41562-024-02024-1. 106 experiments, 370 effect sizes, literature window January 2020 to June 2023; Hedges' g = −0.23 (95% CI −0.39 to −0.07) against the best of human or AI alone; significant moderators include task type and the relative performance of human versus AI alone.

5. Becker, J., Rush, N., Barnes, B., & Rein, D. (2025). "Measuring the impact of early-2025 AI on experienced open-source developer productivity." METR, July 10, 2025. arXiv:2507.09089. See also: Becker, J., Rush, N., Cunningham, T., Rein, D., & Mahamud, K. (2026). "We are changing our developer productivity experiment design." METR, February 24, 2026. https://metr.org/blog/2026-02-24-uplift-update/. The authors treat the 2025 slowdown as a snapshot of early-2025 tools and report that later data is an unreliable signal of the current effect.

6. Fernandes, D., Villa, S., Nicholls, S., Haavisto, O., Buschek, D., Schmidt, A., Kosch, T., Shen, C., & Welsch, R. (2025). "AI makes you smarter but none the wiser: The disconnect between performance and metacognition." *Computers in Human Behavior*, 175, 108779. DOI: 10.1016/j.chb.2025.108779.

7. McKinsey (December 2025). "Redefine AI upskilling as a change imperative." Secondary source reporting findings from Sahni, R. & Chilton, L.B. (2025), arXiv:2502.13281. N=10 qualitative study; the 70% figure is directional.

8. Hermann, E., Puntoni, S., & Morewedge, C.K. (2025). "GenAI and the psychology of work." *Trends in Cognitive Sciences*, 29(9). DOI: 10.1016/j.tics.2025.04.009.

PART I

The Problem Nobody Named

CHAPTER 1

The Gap

Five marketers sit in the same open-plan office on a Tuesday morning. Same Slack channel pinging with the same brief: a consumer electronics company launching a mid-range wireless speaker into a category already crowded with seventeen competitors. The creative director has given everyone two hours to come back with positioning concepts. All five have access to the same AI tool. Same subscription, same model, same capabilities.

By noon, the gap is visible.

Two of them have produced work that is measurably good: positioning built on the brand's actual competitive advantage (a return policy three times more generous than the category leader's), copy aimed at the specific buyer who cares about that advantage, messaging no other agency working this brief would have produced.

The other three have produced work that is polished, grammatically flawless, and strategically empty. "Premium sound meets everyday value." "Designed for the moments that matter." You've read these headlines before. They could sell anything, which means they sell nothing.

Same room. Same tools. Same morning. The two who produced distinctive work brought something into the collaboration that the three didn't: knowledge of this brand's actual competitive position, this audience's actual purchase drivers, this category's dynamics. One of them had spent a week in the brand's customer service queue reading complaints and returns. She knew what buyers cared about because she'd watched them care about it. The AI couldn't have surfaced that. She could, and she used the tool to build on what she already knew. The other three treated AI as something that replaced the need to know.

That gap is what this chapter maps. The numbers are worse than you'd expect.

*

In 2024, the largest analysis of human-AI collaboration ever conducted landed in *Nature Human Behaviour*.

A team led by Michelle Vaccaro at MIT assembled 106 experiments published between January 2020 and June 2023: 370 effect sizes spanning medicine, law, business, and creative work, every domain where researchers had tested what happens when humans and AI work together. The meta-analysis asked the question that the entire AI industry assumes it already knows the answer to: does the combination outperform the best of either one working alone?

The answer was no. Averaged across everything, human-AI combinations performed worse than the better of the two working alone. The effect was modest in size, and the confidence interval sat entirely below zero. The collaboration subtracted value.

Sit with that for a second. Not "failed to add as much as hoped." Subtracted. The largest analysis of human-AI collaboration ever conducted found that putting the two together, on average, produced less than leaving the stronger one alone.

But the average masked enormous variance, and the authors said so: the heterogeneity across studies was high, which is the statistician's way of saying the average is hiding several different stories. Two of them were clear enough to name. The first was task type. On decision tasks, classifying, diagnosing, judging, the combinations lost ground. On content-creation tasks, the combinations gained. The second was who was better to begin with. When the human alone already outperformed the AI alone, adding the AI helped. When the AI alone already outperformed the human, adding the human hurt. Those are two separate moderators, and the paper keeps them separate. A decision task where the human was the stronger party was not the same situation as a decision task where the AI was.

The authors flagged one more thing about their own work, and it's worth carrying: the possibility of publication bias. Studies that find a striking effect get published more readily than studies that don't, and a meta-analysis inherits whatever tilt that creates. They reported the tests they ran. They didn't pretend the tilt away.

Here is what the paper does not prove. It does not prove that the human's mental model is the mechanism. It doesn't measure mental models at all. What it measures is outcomes, and what it finds is that outcomes split along two lines the researchers could see from outside: what kind of task, and who was stronger going in. Anyone who tells you this study proves a psychological theory is reading past the data.

What the paper leaves open is the question this book is about. Look at the second moderator again. The combination gained when there was real human capability to bring, and lost when there wasn't. That's a statement about the human's baseline. It says nothing yet about whether the capable human actually brought their capability into the room. The two marketers who nailed the speaker brief had something the tool couldn't generate, and they used it. Three colleagues with the same tool and, let's assume, comparable careers, didn't. The meta-analysis can tell you the first pair is where the gains live. It can't tell you why the other three left theirs on the table. The rest of this book is one reading of that gap, offered as a reading, and the moderators in the paper leave room for it without requiring it.

A separate research team tried to formalize what productive collaboration would look like. They called it "complementary team performance": each side contributing what the other can't, creating a whole greater than the parts. It's the premise behind every AI implementation pitch deck, every vendor demo, every executive mandate to "adopt AI." When Hemmer and colleagues went looking for this complementarity across the literature, they found it was "rarely observed."

The default outcome of human-AI collaboration, so far, is subtraction. The question the Vaccaro study opens is precise: what distinguishes the cases where it works from the majority where it doesn't?

*

The waste takes a specific form, and the form is what makes it dangerous.

A study of human-robot teams documented a pattern researchers recognized as social loafing, transplanted into a new kind of partnership. When the machine joined the collaboration, humans maintained their motor effort: they kept working, kept producing, kept meeting deadlines. But they reduced their mental effort. The body stays present. The mind steps back. From the outside, it looks like productivity. From the inside, it feels like productivity. The quality degrades so gradually that nobody notices until the output is out the door.

Mid-size consulting firm, about sixty people. The kind of place where the partners still know every client's name, where the senior associates carry ten years of client history in their heads and pride themselves on strategy that reflects it. They roll out AI tools across the strategy team. Six weeks in, the managing partner is reporting usage through the roof. Everyone's using it. Deliverables come in faster. The team is excited. By every metric on the adoption dashboard, the implementation is a success.

Then he pulls three proposals from before the rollout and three from after. Same clients, same scope of work. He reads them side by side. The post-AI proposals are cleaner. Better formatted. More polished. And completely interchangeable. You could swap the client names and nobody would notice. The strategic recommendations could have come from any firm with the same AI subscription. The thing that used to make this firm's proposals worth paying for: deep knowledge of this client's competitive position, this market's dynamics, this industry's unspoken rules? Edited out. Not by the AI. By the humans who stopped contributing it.

His face does that thing: the slow recognition when someone sees a problem they've been looking at without seeing. "They're all the same," he says. And then, quieter: "These could have come from anyone."

That last sentence is the one worth lingering on. A consulting firm's value proposition is that its people know something. They've been inside this client's industry for years. They've seen what works, what doesn't, what the client's competitors tried last quarter that failed in ways the client hasn't heard about yet. That accumulated knowledge is what justifies the fee. Remove it from the deliverable and the deliverable is worth whatever the AI subscription costs. Forty dollars a month, give or take. The firm just commoditized itself.

The managing partner's technology was working exactly as designed. What he had was a collaboration problem: his team had stopped doing the cognitive work that made their output worth paying for, and neither they nor the adoption dashboard had noticed.

Telemetry data makes the same pattern visible at developer scale. In 2025, Faros analyzed productivity across more than ten thousand engineers on over twelve hundred teams, the largest dataset assembled on AI coding tools in real-world conditions. Developers using AI completed 21 percent more tasks. That's the headline everyone wanted. Below the headline: 9 percent more bugs per developer, pull requests 154 percent larger, review times stretched 91 percent longer. CodeRabbit, measuring code quality from a different angle the same year, found roughly 1.7 times more issues in AI-coauthored pull requests than in human-only ones.

And at the company level, the metrics that matter to the business, throughput and quality, the industry-standard DORA measurements? No significant correlation between AI adoption and improvement.

More output. Same or worse outcomes. The bottleneck didn't disappear; it shifted from writing code to reviewing it. Speed at one stage created a pileup at the next. More code, more bugs. The productivity narrative inverted.

Usage is up. Volume is up. Impact is harder to find.

*

If the productivity gap were the whole story, organizations would eventually measure their way to a fix. Track output quality alongside volume. Adjust the workflow. The harder problem lives one layer deeper: the people inside the gap can't see it.

In early 2025, a research organization called METR designed a study that should unsettle anyone who trusts their own judgment about AI. They recruited sixteen experienced open-source developers: people who had been working in their own codebases for an average of five years. Not students. Not novices. Professionals who knew their code the way a carpenter knows the house they've been renovating for a decade, every quirk, every shortcut, every piece of technical debt swept under the rug.

METR randomly assigned AI tools to be available or unavailable for each of 246 real tasks. The developers didn't choose when to use AI. The randomization means the comparison is clean: no self-selection, no "I only use AI for easy tasks" confound. The tools were the best available at the time, Cursor running Claude 3.5 and 3.7.

The result: developers were 19 percent slower with AI tools.

That alone would be worth a conversation. What makes it unsettling is what the developers believed. Before the study, they predicted AI would make them 24 percent faster. After the study, after completing tasks that were objectively measured as taking longer, they still estimated they were 20 percent faster. The gap between what happened and what it felt like happened: roughly 39 percentage points.

Think about what that means. These aren't people unfamiliar with measurement. Developers are trained to think empirically. They write code, run tests, read logs. If experienced developers working in their own codebases can't perceive whether AI is speeding them up or slowing them down, what does that say about the rest of us evaluating our AI-assisted work on gut feel?

Now the part that most people who quote this study leave out. In February 2026, the same researchers published an update, and it's a model of how to be honest about your own headline. They no longer treat the 19 percent as a description of the present. The tools had changed too much. They'd tried to run a second wave and hit a wall: somewhere between 30 and 50 percent of participants told them they were declining to submit tasks they didn't want to do without AI. When people refuse the no-AI condition, the comparison is no longer clean. Based on what participants told them, the researchers said they believe developers are probably sped up by AI now. They also said their later data is an unreliable signal of how much.

So what survives? Not "AI makes experts slower." That was one measurement of one set of tools in one season, and the people who took it have said so. What survives is the thing the tools can't fix: sixteen professionals were wrong about their own speed by roughly forty points, in the same direction, and stayed wrong after the measurement was done. The load-bearing finding was never the slowdown. It was the miscalibration.

And that part shows up wherever it's been looked for so far.

Fernandes and colleagues tested whether AI literacy, how much someone understands about how AI works, correlates with better collaboration outcomes. You'd expect it would. More knowledge should produce better judgment. The finding went the other direction: higher AI literacy correlated with lower metacognitive accuracy. The people who understood AI the best were the worst at evaluating their own performance with it. One study; treat it as a flag, not a law. But read it again anyway. The people who know the most about AI misjudge their own AI-assisted work the most.

I love that finding. Not because it's cheerful; it's the opposite. I love it because it complicates a door that a lot of organizations want to walk through without looking: the door marked "just train people better." If the problem were ignorance, knowledge would fix it. This finding, if it holds, says knowledge makes the self-assessment worse. Which puts the problem somewhere else entirely, and suggests that some of the billions we're spending on AI training are building confidence without building the thing confidence is supposed to rest on.

None of this is a discovery about AI. Psychologists have known for decades that people misjudge their own competence, and that the misjudgment runs in a predictable direction: the less skilled overestimate more. They've known that people underestimate how long their own projects will take, then do it again on the next project. The planning fallacy and the Dunning-Kruger effect are the simpler cousins of what METR measured. What's new is the amplifier. Those older biases operated on work whose quality you could at least inspect. AI produces work whose polish has come loose from its correctness, and polish is the signal every one of us was trained to check first. The old miscalibration had friction working against it. This one has fluency working for it.

A BambooHR survey found that 70 percent of workers who believed they could spot AI-generated content got it wrong. Li and colleagues found that when an AI displayed high confidence, only 26 percent of participants noticed the confidence was unwarranted; most read it as appropriate, and overconfident AI led people to switch to bad advice because it sounded sure of itself. The gap between performance and self-assessment is the signature of the problem, and it shows up well beyond one study with sixteen developers. And it creates a specific organizational consequence: if you measure AI success by asking people whether they feel more productive, you're measuring confidence, not competence. The Faros telemetry is the organizational version of the METR story, task counts climbing over a floor of bugs and review time. Output volume is not productivity.

*

The reason the perception gap persists is structural. It has a name: the fluency trap.

AI produces output that matches every surface signal professionals use to evaluate quality. It's articulate. Confident. Well-structured. Complete. The sentences cohere. The formatting is clean. These are the signals that experienced professionals have spent careers using as proxies for "this work is good." When the output matches those signals, the normal quality-checking instincts say it's fine.

But the signals have been decoupled from the thing they used to indicate. Polish no longer means accuracy. Confidence no longer means correctness. Coherence no longer means rigor. The heuristics that AI is best at mimicking are exactly the ones humans rely on most. The trap is that AI produces work that looks good by every standard we've trained ourselves to apply, whether or not the work is actually good.

Picture reviewing two drafts of a market analysis. Draft A is rough: incomplete sentences, placeholder citations, visible gaps in the logic. Draft B is polished: confident assertions, smooth transitions, professional formatting. Your brain reads Draft A as "needs work" and Draft B as "mostly done." But what if Draft B's confident assertions are wrong? What if the smooth transitions hide logical gaps that Draft A's roughness would have forced you to confront? AI produces Draft B every time. That's the fluency trap: the quality signals you've always relied on are no longer reliable.

And the trap doesn't just distort evaluation. It erodes capability.

Wharton researchers ran an experiment with roughly a thousand high school students, giving them access to ChatGPT for practice problems in mathematics. Some got unrestricted access: type any question, get any answer. Others got a tutor version that offered hints and asked questions back instead of handing over solutions. During practice, both groups improved. The unrestricted group improved by 48 percent. The tutor group improved by 127 percent, more than double, because the harder path maintained cognitive engagement.

Then the AI was taken away.

The unrestricted group didn't just lose what they'd gained. They performed 17 percent below students who had never had the tool at all. The easy path hadn't merely failed to build capability. It had eroded the capability they started with. The tutor group showed no deskilling. The mechanism, in the researchers' own framing, was a crutch: an unfettered model that would hand over the answer got used as one.

Same tool, same students, same content. The only variable was how much thinking the collaboration demanded from the human. The easy path felt productive and created dependency. The hard path felt like work and created capability. Robert Bjork named this thirty years ago in the learning literature, before anyone was typing into a chatbot: the difficulties that feel like obstacles during practice are often the ones doing the teaching. He called them desirable difficulties. The Wharton experiment is what it looks like when a tool removes them.

One honest boundary. Those were teenagers doing algebra, and no one has run the equivalent trial on a boardroom. That a securities attorney or a strategy consultant deskills the same way, on the same timeline, by the same mechanism, is a theoretical extension of the finding, not a demonstrated one. It's a reasonable extension; the mechanism doesn't obviously care what the subject matter is. But reasonable is the right word, and this book will use it.

A randomized study of 120 undergraduates points the same direction. Forty-five days after studying with ChatGPT, on a surprise retention test they didn't know was coming, the AI-using group scored 57.5 percent. The control group, working without AI, scored 68.5 percent. The tool had done the work, and the work hadn't stayed.

What makes these findings so difficult is that they describe a trap with no obvious exit. The polish of AI output disables the quality checks that would catch the problem. The ease of AI collaboration discourages the effort that would prevent deskilling. And the perception gap means the people inside the trap believe they're performing well. They're cutting corners they can't see. The trap is a systematic mismatch between how AI output looks and what it delivers, between how AI collaboration feels and what it does to the human's capability over time.

*

Corporate America's response to all of this has been to train people harder.

Corporate learning is a four-hundred-billion-dollar industry, and a growing share of it now aims at AI. Companies ran workshops, built onboarding programs, hired consultants to teach teams how to use the tools. A small Columbia study that McKinsey amplified in late 2025 tells you how that landed: seven of the ten Copilot users the researchers interviewed never watched the onboarding videos.

Think about why. You know what this looks like. You get an email from IT: mandatory AI training, thirty minutes, click here. A narrator explains what a large language model is. There's a slide about prompting best practices. There's a quiz that tests whether you remember the definition of "hallucination." You pass. You close the tab. Nothing about how you work tomorrow is different from how you worked yesterday.

Ten people is a vignette, not a statistic. It sticks because everyone recognizes the behavior. The people who close the tab have correctly sensed that a video about how the tool works won't change anything about how they relate to the tool. Their intuition is better than the intervention design.

For the people who do engage with the training, the news isn't better. BCG's 2025 data shows that employees with five or more hours of AI training are more likely to be regular AI users: 79 percent versus 67 percent for those with less. Training increases usage. But usage without impact is the problem this chapter has been documenting from its opening paragraph. The training succeeded at the wrong metric.

MIT's GenAI research initiative studied a hundred and fifty leaders, surveyed three hundred and fifty employees, and analyzed three hundred public AI deployments. Roughly 5 percent of pilot programs achieved rapid revenue acceleration. Five percent. Take it as directional rather than as a law, but nineteen out of twenty companies that ran AI pilots got nothing they could point to. The UK government's AI incubator, i.AI, tested fifty-seven ideas in its first year. Eleven reached the development pipeline. Twenty-two more sat in incubation. The rest went nowhere. Even a cross-departmental team built specifically to make this work confirmed the pattern: pilots are easy, impact is rare.

Then there's Microsoft, the company that renamed half its product line to include the word "Copilot." When it reported earnings in January 2026, analysts put the paid Copilot base at roughly 15 million seats against 450 million commercial Microsoft 365 users: about 3 percent. By April the company was reporting more than 20 million. The number will keep moving, and any figure printed in a book is a snapshot. What the snapshots share is the shape: the company with more distribution power than almost anyone on the planet has converted a small slice of the people who already had the product at hand. The reason is telling. In a 2025 survey of people who had tried Copilot and quit, 44 percent said they stopped because they didn't trust the answers. They tried to collaborate, couldn't tell when it was right, and walked away.

Think about the consulting firm from a few pages back. Those strategists had training. They knew how the tools worked. They could prompt effectively, format outputs, integrate AI into their workflow: all the skills a training program teaches. And they still produced interchangeable proposals. The thing that makes a proposal worth reading isn't something a training program delivers. It's the judgment, the pattern recognition, the willingness to say "this is wrong for this client" that comes from knowing your domain deeply enough to push back. Training teaches you how to operate the tool. It doesn't teach you how to stay present while you're operating it. And staying present turns out to be the entire game.

Usage without impact. Training without behavior change. Adoption without the thing adoption was supposed to produce.

*

By now the objection is forming, and it deserves better than a brush-off: sometimes the tool is the problem.

It is. Google's Gemini shipped historically absurd images in 2024 and had to pull the feature. Air Canada's website chatbot invented a bereavement-fare policy, a grieving customer relied on it, and a Canadian tribunal held the airline to what its software had promised. In 2023 two New York lawyers filed a brief citing six cases that did not exist, because a chatbot had produced them with docket numbers and quotations, and a federal judge sanctioned them for it. None of those failures were subtle once someone looked. All of them got out the door because the output was fluent and nobody did.

Here's what those cases are. They're fluency-trap cases: verification failed because the surface signals said it didn't need to. They are also a limit on this book's argument, because they show that psychology is a large part of the story and never the whole of it. Sometimes the model is wrong on a task it should get right, and no amount of expertise entering the collaboration fixes a fabricated docket number. Sometimes the data it was given is bad. Sometimes the risk of a confident error is unacceptable for the task at hand, and the correct amount of AI is none.

So the reader who has been sorting themselves into "fight mode" since the Introduction should pause. Refusing to use a tool for a task it fails at is not fight. It's calibration. The difference is the reason, and the reason is testable. The fighter refuses on identity grounds: the tool threatens something about who they are, so it's wrong for everything, and evidence that it did well on a task doesn't move them. The calibrated skeptic refuses on evidence: it fabricated citations, so it's out for citations, and it's back in for the summary it did well on last week. One position updates. The other doesn't. You can tell them apart by asking what would change your mind.

That means calibration includes moves that look, from outside, like resistance. Switching to a different tool for a task the first one keeps missing. Narrowing what you ask for until the tool is inside its competence. Adding a verification step that costs you the time you were hoping to save. Not opening the model at all for the memo where a fluent error would cost you a client. Every one of those is a high-engagement choice by someone who has a working model of what the tool can do. A senior attorney who runs every AI-surfaced citation through the docket before it touches a filing isn't fighting the tool. She's the reason the tool is safe to use.

Which is why this book will not treat every disappointing output as a failure of the human. Some misses are the tool. The question that separates the cases is whether the person could have known, and whether they checked. The lawyers who filed the fake citations were asked by the judge whether they'd verified the cases. They hadn't. That's the fluency trap. A lawyer who verified, found the cases missing, and stopped using the tool for research: that's the relationship working.

But grant all of that and the larger pattern still stands. The same tools that fabricate citations produce extraordinary work for somebody every day. The meta-analysis didn't find that AI was weak; it found that the combination was, and it found the gains sitting right there in the same data, in the hands of people who brought more. The METR developers weren't holding broken tools;

they were holding state-of-the-art tools and misreading what happened. If the technology were the constraint, waiting would fix it. The technology has improved every quarter since 2022, and the gap between what it can do and what most people get from it hasn't closed.

*

The five marketers are still in that room.

The two who produced distinctive work didn't have better prompts or more training hours. They had something that training programs don't teach and AI subscriptions don't include: specific knowledge of this brand, this audience, this competitive landscape, and the habit of bringing that knowledge into the collaboration rather than letting the tool work around it. The marketer who'd spent a week in the customer service queue brought something into the process that the AI couldn't generate and the other three didn't contribute. That's the variable.

Every finding in this chapter points to the same place. The Vaccaro meta-analysis didn't discover that AI was incapable; it found gains where the human had something real to bring and losses where they didn't, and it left open what decides whether the capable human brings it. The METR developers weren't using broken tools; they were misreading their own performance with functioning ones. The students in the Wharton-run study didn't lack access to AI; they lacked the cognitive engagement that turns access into capability. The consulting firm's strategy team didn't produce interchangeable proposals because their AI was bad; they produced them because nobody brought the thing that makes a proposal worth reading: knowledge of this client that no subscription provides.

In every case, the technology performed. The collaboration didn't. The gap lives in the space between the person and the tool: the space where expertise either enters the collaboration or doesn't, where judgment either sharpens against AI's output or dissolves into it, where the human either stays cognitively present or quietly checks out.

That space has a history, and this book didn't discover it. Technology-acceptance research has modeled the human-technology relationship for decades. TAM, UTAUT, the Technology Readiness Index: they explain, with hundreds of validating studies behind them, why people pick up new tools or don't. Perceived usefulness, ease of use, social influence, readiness. They work. But they model the adoption decision: will you use it? Parasuraman and Riley, in the automation literature, went one step further in 1997 and named what happens after yes: misuse and disuse, too much reliance and too little. What they didn't do is explain which one a given person lands on, or why an expert who understands the tool perfectly still withholds the expertise that would make it useful. The gap this chapter documents lives downstream of adoption, in the during-use space: how much of your capability actually enters the collaboration, how accurately you read the tool's contribution, whether the interaction builds your expertise or erodes it. This book's argument is that identity and self-efficacy often decide that, and the coming chapters make the case.

The during-use space is where the value gets created or destroyed. It also gets a fraction of the attention that adoption gets. Organizations pour resources into the adoption question: selecting tools, training people, mandating usage, measuring uptake. The dashboards track who's using AI and how often. Few of them track what happens to the quality of thinking while the tool is in use, or whether the human contribution is entering the collaboration or being quietly edited out. The consulting firm's managing partner didn't discover the problem on a dashboard. He discovered it by reading proposals.

If the problem were knowledge, training would fix it. If it were technology, better models would fix it. Neither has. The tools keep getting more capable; the gap between what they can do and what people get from them keeps growing. Something else is going on, something that lives in the relationship between the person and the tool, in how people see themselves when they sit down to collaborate with a machine that can do parts of their job.

So what does a productive relationship with AI actually look like? What separates the two marketers who produced distinctive work from the three who produced noise, and can that difference be taught, or is it something people either bring or they don't? Why does everything we're currently spending, the billions in training, the prompt libraries, the change management consultants, keep aiming at the wrong layer?

Every one of those is a question about people. The next chapter starts on what people have already tried.

Notes

1. Vaccaro, M., Almaatouq, A., & Malone, T. (2024). "When combinations of humans and AI are useful: A systematic review and meta-analysis." *Nature Human Behaviour*, 8(12), 2293-2303. DOI: 10.1038/s41562-024-02024-1. Preprint: arXiv:2405.06087. Preregistered; 106 experiments, 370 effect sizes, literature window January 2020 to June 2023. Human-AI combinations versus the best of human or AI alone: Hedges' g = −0.23 (95% CI −0.39 to −0.07). Losses on decision tasks, gains on content-creation tasks; gains when the human alone outperformed the AI alone, losses when the AI alone outperformed the human. High heterogeneity; the authors report tests for publication bias as a limitation.
2. Hemmer, P., Schemmer, M., Kühl, N., Vössing, M., & Satzger, G. (2025). "Complementarity in human-AI collaboration: Concept, sources, and evidence." *European Journal of Information Systems*, 34(6), 979-1002. DOI: 10.1080/0960085X.2025.2475962.
3. Cymek, D.H., Truckenbrodt, A., & Onnasch, L. (2023). "Lean back or lean in? Exploring social loafing in human-robot teams." *Frontiers in Robotics and AI*, 10, 1249252. DOI: 10.3389/frobt.2023.1249252. Source for the "maintained motor effort but reduced mental effort" finding.
4. Faros AI (2025). "The AI Productivity Paradox: AI Coding Assistants Increase Developer Output, But Not Company Productivity." Published July 23, 2025. 10,000+ developers, 1,255 teams; 21% more tasks, 9% more bugs per developer, PRs 154% larger, review time +91%; no significant correlation between AI adoption and company-level DORA metrics.
5. CodeRabbit (2025). "State of AI vs Human Code Generation Report." Published December 17, 2025. Analysis of 470 open-source GitHub pull

requests; AI-co-authored PRs contained ~1.7x more issues than human-only PRs.

6. Becker, J., Rush, N., Barnes, B., & Rein, D. (2025). "Measuring the impact of early-2025 AI on experienced open-source developer productivity." METR, July 10, 2025. arXiv:2507.09089. https://metr.org/blog/2025-07-10-early-2025-ai-experienced-os-dev-study. 16 developers, 246 tasks, Cursor with Claude 3.5/3.7; +19% completion time with AI; predicted −24% before, estimated −20% after.
7. Becker, J., Rush, N., Cunningham, T., Rein, D., & Mahamud, K. (2026). "We are changing our developer productivity experiment design." METR, February 24, 2026. https://metr.org/blog/2026-02-24-uplift-update/. The authors report that 30–50% of later-wave participants declined to submit tasks they did not want to do without AI, state they believe developers are likely more sped up in early 2026 than in early 2025, and describe their later data as an unreliable signal of the size of that effect.
8. Fernandes, D., Villa, S., Nicholls, S., Haavisto, O., Buschek, D., Schmidt, A., Kosch, T., Shen, C., & Welsch, R. (2025). "AI makes you smarter but none the wiser: The disconnect between performance and metacognition." *Computers in Human Behavior*, 175, 108779. DOI: 10.1016/j.chb.2025.108779. Single study.
9. Kruger, J. & Dunning, D. (1999). "Unskilled and unaware of it: How difficulties in recognizing one's own incompetence lead to inflated self-assessments." *Journal of Personality and Social Psychology*, 77(6), 1121-1134. Kahneman, D. & Tversky, A. (1979). "Intuitive prediction: Biases and corrective procedures." *TIMS Studies in Management Science*, 12, 313-327. Source of the planning fallacy.
10. BambooHR (2025). "Think You Can Spot AI? Think Again: 70% of Workers Get It Wrong." Conducted with Method Research.
11. Li, J., Yang, Y., Zhang, R., Liao, Q.V., Song, T., Xu, Z., & Lee, Y. (2024). "Understanding the effects of miscalibrated AI confidence on user trust, reliance, and decision efficacy." *CHI 2024*. arXiv:2402.07632. 26% of participants correctly perceived overconfidence; overconfident AI raised switch rates to its advice.
12. Bastani, H., Bastani, O., Sungu, A., Ge, H., Kabakcı, Ö., & Mariman, R. (2025). "Generative AI without guardrails can harm learning: Evidence from high school mathematics." *Proceedings of the National Academy of Sciences*, 122(26), e2422633122. DOI: 10.1073/pnas.2422633122. High-school mathematics; GPT-4; GPT Base vs GPT Tutor vs control. Practice: Base +48%, Tutor +127%. After removal: Base −17% versus never-AI; Tutor no deskilling.
13. Bjork, R.A. (1994). "Memory and metamemory considerations in the training of human beings." In J. Metcalfe & A.P. Shimamura (Eds.), *Metacognition: Knowing About Knowing* (pp. 185-205). MIT Press. Source of "desirable difficulties."

14. Barcaui, A. (2025). "ChatGPT as a cognitive crutch: Evidence from a randomized controlled trial on knowledge retention." *Social Sciences & Humanities Open*, 12, 102287. DOI: 10.1016/j.ssaho.2025.102287. N=120; 45-day retention 57.5% (AI) vs 68.5% (control).

15. Bersin, J. (2026). "New Research: How AI Transforms $400 Billion of Corporate Learning." joshbersin.com, February 2026.

16. McKinsey (December 2025). "Redefine AI upskilling as a change imperative." Secondary source reporting findings from Sahni, R. & Chilton, L.B. (2025). "Beyond AI Training: How Social and Experiential Learning Shape AI Adoption in the Workplace." Columbia University. arXiv:2502.13281. N=10 qualitative study; the figure is directional.

17. BCG (2025). "AI Adoption Puzzle: Why Usage Is Up But Impact Is Not." 79% regular use among employees with 5+ hours of training vs 67% with less.

18. MIT NANDA (2025). "The GenAI Divide: State of AI in Business 2025." July 2025. 150 leader interviews, 350-employee survey, 300 public deployments analyzed; ~5% of pilots achieved rapid revenue acceleration. Directional industry evidence.

19. Gilbert, L. (2024). "One Year of i.AI: Reimagining Government through Artificial Intelligence." i.AI Blog, 16 December 2024. https://ai.gov.uk/blogs/one-year-of-iai-reimagining-government-through-artificial-intelligence/.

20. Microsoft earnings disclosures, FY2026 Q2 (January 28, 2026: ~15 million paid Microsoft 365 Copilot seats against a ~450-million commercial base, as reported by Directions on Microsoft, Windows Central, and Computerworld) and FY2026 Q3 (April 29, 2026: "over 20 million" paid seats; paid M365 commercial seats +6% year over year). Recon Analytics survey data (2025): 44% of lapsed Copilot users cited distrust of answers; accuracy Net Promoter Score declined from −3.5 (July 2025) to −24.1 (September 2025). All figures are dated snapshots.

21. Google Gemini image-generation failures, February 2024; multiple news sources.

22. *Moffatt v. Air Canada*, British Columbia Civil Resolution Tribunal, February 2024. Airline held liable for incorrect bereavement-fare information provided by its website chatbot.

23. *Mata v. Avianca, Inc.*, No. 22-cv-1461 (S.D.N.Y. June 22, 2023), sanctions order. Attorneys sanctioned for filing a brief citing six nonexistent cases generated by ChatGPT.

24. Davis, F.D. (1989). "Perceived usefulness, perceived ease of use, and user acceptance of information technology." *MIS Quarterly*, 13(3), 319-340.

25. Venkatesh, V., Morris, M.G., Davis, G.B., & Davis, F.D. (2003). "User acceptance of information technology: Toward a unified view." *MIS Quarterly*, 27(3), 425-478.

26. Parasuraman, A. (2000). "Technology Readiness Index (TRI): A multiple-item scale to measure readiness to embrace new technologies." *Journal of Service Research*, 2(4), 307-320. DOI: 10.1177/109467050024001.

27. Parasuraman, R. & Riley, V. (1997). "Humans and automation: Use, misuse, disuse, abuse." *Human Factors*, 39(2), 230-253.

CHAPTER 2

What We Tried Instead

A director of strategy at a mid-size professional services firm has completed three AI certification programs in the past eighteen months. She can explain transformer architecture. She can list the differences between GPT-4 and Claude, debate the ethics of training data at industry conferences, and she published a LinkedIn post about responsible AI adoption that got four hundred likes. Her employer considers her the team's AI champion. She uses AI daily. Her deliverables haven't improved.

Every morning she opens ChatGPT, types a request, reviews the output, cleans it up, and sends it forward. The proposals look polished. The strategic recommendations read well. But pull three of them side by side and a pattern emerges: they could have come from anyone with the same subscription. The specificity that used to distinguish her work – the pattern recognition built from eight years in this industry, the intuition about which competitive dynamics actually matter for this client – none of it enters the collaboration. Her knowledge about AI is real. Her relationship with AI hasn't changed.

She is the training industry's ideal graduate. She knows more about AI than 95 percent of her peers. And she operates exactly the same way as someone who took no training at all: type a request, accept what comes back.

*

The field has tried, hard. The people building AI training programs, teaching prompt engineering, and running change management playbooks aren't wrong about the problem. They're wrong about the layer. And the distinction matters, because the interventions they've built do real things: they increase adoption, they improve initial engagement, they reduce the fear factor. What they don't do is change the relationship between the person and the tool. And the relationship, as Chapter 1 established, is where the value gets created or destroyed.

Three dominant responses have emerged to the AI collaboration gap. Each one addresses something real. Each one misses the same thing. And anyone who's tried to lead AI adoption in their organization will recognize all three, because most organizations have tried all three, often simultaneously, and arrived at the same place: more usage, same results.

*

The first response is education: teach people about AI and they'll use it well.

The assumption is intuitive. If people don't collaborate effectively with AI, it must be because they don't understand it well enough. Build their knowledge. Explain how models work, where they hallucinate, what they're good at. The multibillion-dollar AI training industry runs on this logic, and the logic is sound as far as it goes. It doesn't go far enough.

AI literacy has genuine value. Understanding that large language models predict text rather than "knowing" things helps you interpret outputs more critically. Knowing where hallucinations cluster helps you target your verification efforts. Understanding capability boundaries helps you choose the right tool for the right task. None of this is worthless. The problem is that most of the AI training industry treats literacy as the destination when it's barely the starting line.

The evidence is uncomfortable, and worth sitting with.

Fernandes and colleagues tested whether AI literacy correlated with better collaboration outcomes. You'd expect it would. More knowledge should produce better judgment. But the relationship went the other direction: higher AI literacy correlated with lower metacognitive accuracy. The most knowledgeable AI users overestimated the quality of their own AI-assisted work the most. And the majority of participants rarely asked more than one question per problem, regardless of how much they knew about AI. The single-interaction pattern persisted across literacy levels.

That last finding is easy to skip past, but it's the one that should keep training designers up at night. The single-interaction pattern means that the people who know the most about AI still treat it the same way as the people who know the least: ask once, accept the answer, move on. The knowledge changed. The behavior didn't. If knowledge drove behavior, the most literate users would iterate more, push back more, bring more of their own thinking into the interaction. They don't. Something else is driving the pattern, and it's not something a certification program can reach.

BambooHR's detection data from Chapter 1 makes the related point: 70 percent of workers who believed they could spot AI-generated content got it wrong. If people can't reliably detect AI output, which is the simpler task, evaluating its quality is further out of reach than anyone running a training program wants to admit.

The Dunning-Kruger effect is the obvious explanation, and it deserves honest acknowledgment. People overestimate their ability in domains where the feedback signals are ambiguous. That's a well-documented, domain-general bias. But AI collaboration has a specific feature that makes the bias worse: the fluency trap. In most domains, bad work looks bad. A poorly written brief reads poorly. A flawed analysis produces visible errors. AI output doesn't work that way. It's polished, coherent, and confident regardless of whether it's accurate. The quality signals we've spent our careers learning to read, the ones that tell us "this is solid work" or "this needs revision," stop functioning as reliability indicators. General metacognitive bias doesn't explain that on its own. It's a feature of AI collaboration specifically, and literacy training can't reach it, because the training targets knowledge while the failure happens at the level of judgment under deceptive conditions.

BCG's data closes the loop. Workers with five or more hours of AI training were more likely to be regular AI users: 79 percent, compared to 67 percent for those with less training. Training drives adoption. But the organizational pattern that Chapter 1 documented (usage up, impact flat) persists regardless of training hours. The training succeeded at its own metric. The metric was the wrong one.

Think about what that means for the L&D director who just ran a six-month AI literacy program. She can point to higher adoption numbers. She can show survey data proving that her people feel more confident with AI tools. And she's watching the same pattern Chapter 1 documented: the work product hasn't changed. Her program succeeded. Her organization didn't benefit. The program was aimed at the wrong thing.

None of this means training is worthless. It means training is insufficient as a standalone intervention, and the field treats it as sufficient. The director of strategy who completed three certification programs has been trained thoroughly, at the wrong layer. Her knowledge about AI is extensive. Her mental model for working with AI, the assumptions about her role in the collaboration and what she brings that the tool can't generate alone, hasn't shifted.

*

The second response is technique: learn the right prompts and you'll get good outputs.

Prompt engineering workshops proliferated faster than any other AI training format. The appeal is obvious: prompting is actionable. You can teach someone a framework in an afternoon, and by the end of the session they're getting better results from the tool. The immediate feedback loop makes it feel like progress.

The problem is perishability. Model updates change how AI interprets instructions, which formatting it prefers, which techniques produce which outputs. A chain-of-thought pattern optimized for one model version often produces different or worse results on the next. The cycle is quarterly at minimum. A company that runs a prompt engineering workshop in January can expect half the specific techniques to degrade by March.

Picture a team of analysts after that January workshop. They've learned specific formatting tricks, chain-of-thought patterns, system prompts that produce cleaner outputs. For six weeks, the techniques work. Then the model updates. The analysts who memorized templates are stuck: they're trying to use syntax that the new model handles natively, or interprets differently, or ignores entirely. The analysts who never memorized templates in the first place — the ones who brought their domain knowledge into the interaction regardless of prompt format — didn't notice the update. Their work continued without interruption, because what they contributed wasn't tool-specific. It was expertise-specific.

This is where the critique needs precision. The prompting paradigm as typically taught (memorize templates, learn syntax tricks, follow formulas) produces perishable, tool-specific skills. That version of prompting frames the human as an operator: someone who drives the tool by giving it correct instructions. Operators optimize their technique. When the technique expires, so does their effectiveness.

But the best prompt engineers aren't doing this at all. They're bringing deep domain knowledge, specific judgment, and real context into every interaction. What they do isn't "prompting" in the way the industry teaches it. A financial analyst who provides her own hypothesis, her knowledge of this client's risk profile, and the specific anomalies she noticed in last quarter's data is contributing expertise the tool couldn't generate alone. A lawyer who brings the judge's prior rulings, the opposing counsel's documented patterns, and her own strategic theory of the case is shaping the collaboration, not operating a machine.

That kind of engagement is the behavioral expression of what this book will call Condition 1: seeing yourself as the essential contributor. The best prompt engineers are already practicing this, whether or not they'd call it that. The mechanism is clear: the quality of the output tracks the quality of the human contribution, and the prompt syntax is incidental. Their skill transfers across model updates because it was never tool-specific in the first place.

The distinction becomes visible when you watch two people with the same prompt engineering training work on the same problem. One follows the template: role assignment, structured instructions, output format specification. She gets back a clean, professional deliverable that reads like it could have come from any competent professional with the same subscription. The other brings something the template can't contain: her knowledge that this particular client's board is skeptical of international expansion because of a failed acquisition three years ago, her read on why the CFO's questions in the last meeting signaled budget anxiety rather than strategic doubt, her judgment that the competitive threat everyone's focused on is the wrong one. The template is identical. The output is unrecognizable. What separates them is what the second person brought to the table that the tool couldn't have generated on its own.

Which is worth pausing on. The prompting paradigm isn't wrong about what works. It's wrong about what makes it work. The industry teaches syntax when the mechanism is contribution quality. And contribution quality can't be taught in a template workshop, because it depends on having something worth contributing: domain expertise, contextual knowledge, professional judgment. Those are skills the person already has. The question is whether those skills enter the collaboration or stay in the person's head while they type generic requests.

*

The third response is process management: manage the rollout correctly and people will adapt.

Change management is a mature discipline with real theoretical depth. Bridges' Transition Model addresses the psychological loss inherent in change. ADKAR includes desire and reinforcement as core components. Prosci's methodology has emotional readiness elements built into its framework. The discipline contains the concepts for addressing the human side of technology adoption. The problem is that the median corporate AI rollout doesn't execute them.

What organizations actually deploy is a communication plan, a timeline, executive sponsorship, training sessions, department champions, a dedicated support channel, and a phased rollout. All of these address real friction. None of them touch the specific mechanism that makes AI different from every other tool adoption that came before.

When a company migrated from one CRM to another, the change management challenge was operational: new workflows, new data entry habits, new reporting structures. Painful, but the nature of the work didn't change. A sales rep was still a sales rep. The tool upgrade never raised the question of whether the rep's judgment was still necessary. AI raises it. Using it well forces a person to confront a question about their own professional value that a CRM migration never asked, and a process can't answer a question like that.

Here's what that looks like in practice. Mid-size professional services firm, about a hundred people. They execute a textbook change management process for their AI rollout. Executive sponsor engaged. Communications clear and frequent. Phased rollout. Monthly training. Champions in every department. Six months in, the adoption metrics look excellent. Usage is up. The support channel is quiet, which the project team reads as "things are going well." Leadership declares success.

Nine months in, a quieter pattern surfaces. Senior consultants use AI for administrative tasks: scheduling, email drafts, internal documentation. They avoid it for client-facing work. When asked why, the answers are surface-level: "It's not there yet for strategic work." "I prefer my own process for client deliverables." The real reason, visible in candid one-on-ones but never captured in any change management dashboard: using AI for the strategic work that defines their professional value feels like admitting that twenty years of expertise isn't sufficient. The rollout addressed every process barrier. It never touched the identity barrier.

This isn't a hypothetical vulnerability. Mirbabaie and colleagues established that identity threat operates as an independent adoption barrier for AI. Their research identified three central predictors: changes to work, loss of status or position, and what they called "AI identity," how individuals see themselves in relation to AI. The critical word is "independent." Identity threat is a distinct psychological phenomenon, separable from generic change-resistance. You can solve the knowledge problem and the process problem and still have the identity problem, because it runs on its own channel.

The social dimension makes it structural, not just personal. Reif, Larrick, and Soll ran four preregistered experiments with a total of 4,439 participants and found that using AI resulted in a 9 percent lower competence rating from peers. The penalty was steeper for women in engineering: 13 percent. And when male non-adopters evaluated female colleagues who used AI, the competence penalty hit 26 percent. A career tax, paid for using the tool the organization presumably wants you to use. When the social environment punishes AI adoption at that scale, resistance is a rational response to a real cost. No communication plan overcomes a competence penalty that steep. No executive sponsorship reverses a social cost that concrete.

Think about what that 26 percent means for a woman engineer deciding whether to mention that she used AI to prototype a solution. She's making a career calculation, weighing the efficiency gain against a social penalty that's been measured, documented, and published. When people call that resistance, they're describing a symptom. The cause is an environment that punishes exactly the behavior the rollout was designed to encourage.

Which is why 79 percent of organizations now report AI adoption challenges, a double-digit increase from the prior year. Two years of change management hasn't reduced the problem. It's intensifying. If the standard approach worked, the numbers would be improving with experience. They're moving the other direction.

The discipline of change management has the theoretical tools to address identity. The practice, as most organizations execute it, doesn't. Bridges wrote about the difference between change and transition: change is situational, transition is psychological. ADKAR's "desire" component is supposed to address motivation at the individual level, not just organizational compliance. But the median AI rollout collapses "desire" into "we showed them the productivity gains and they should want this now." Which assumes the psychological side will take care of itself once the rational case is made.

The discipline of change management has known for decades that identity matters in organizational change. What's been missing is the specific mechanism: professional identity threat, operating independently of knowledge and process factors, requiring an intervention specific enough to address how a person sees their professional worth in relation to a tool that can perform parts of their job. "Address the psychological side" is the discipline's guidance. Without that precision, the guidance is too vague to be actionable when the psychological side involves a person's fundamental sense of what makes them valuable.

*

Step back from the individual failures and two behavioral responses come into focus. Every organization that's tried to adopt AI has seen both of them. They look opposite on the surface. They share a root.

The first mode is surrender. Accept every output. Edit lightly. Ship fast. The body stays present; the mind checks out. This book's term for it: "algorithmic loafing," social loafing transplanted into the human-AI partnership. In studies of human-AI teamwork, participants maintained motor effort but reduced mental effort when AI joined the collaboration. They kept working. They stopped thinking. Parasuraman and Riley documented the pattern in 1997 under the name "misuse," studying pilots and industrial automation operators. Nearly thirty years later, the same pattern plays out at every desk with a ChatGPT subscription.

The second mode is fight. Override every recommendation. Rewrite every draft from scratch. Treat every AI suggestion as evidence that the tool doesn't understand. Reactance theory, formulated by Brehm in 1966, describes what happens when people perceive a threat to their autonomy: they push back, often harder than the threat warrants. AI triggers reactance when it encroaches on work that defines professional identity. The senior partner who'll let AI handle document review but won't allow it near case strategy is protecting the territory where his expertise lives, and from where he stands that is a reasonable thing to do. The cost is invisible to him: he'll never discover the patterns AI could have surfaced, the blind spots his experience creates as well as covers.

Both responses are rational given an inadequate mental model. Surrender makes sense if you believe AI is the capable one and your contribution doesn't matter much. Fight makes sense if you believe AI threatens who you are and what you've built. Both produce the same result: the tool's potential, wasted.

Automation bias research covers the surrender side. Reactance theory covers the fight side. What neither framework captures on its own is that the two modes share a root. They look like opposite problems requiring opposite solutions. They're two expressions of the same underlying gap: the absence of a productive model for what the human's role in the collaboration actually is. Surrender says "AI does the work." Fight says "I do the work." Neither says "we produce something together that neither could produce alone."

A distinction matters here, because the healthy middle isn't "question everything." Rational delegation, deliberately assigning AI tasks you could do but choose not to because your judgment isn't the differentiating factor, is healthy. A senior consultant who asks AI to compile market sizing data while she focuses on competitive positioning is making a smart allocation decision. Surrender is abdicating judgment on tasks that require it. Delegation is allocating tasks that don't. The difference is whether you chose what to delegate based on where your judgment adds value or based on what you didn't feel like thinking about.

Fight doesn't always argue. Some of it withdraws. The professional who never says a word against the tool and never opens it either is protecting the same territory as the one who overrides every recommendation, just more quietly. Quiet opt-out is treated here as fight expressed through withdrawal rather than argument; the same identity-protective mechanism is at work.

Most people don't stay in one mode. They oscillate. A consultant starts a client project with enthusiasm: "AI will handle the initial research." He pastes in the brief, gets back a twelve-page output that looks thorough but misses the client's actual competitive dynamics. Disappointed, he switches to fight mode, rewrites the analysis from scratch, and spends twice as long as he would have without the tool. Two weeks later, drowning in deliverables, he switches back to surrender: "Just give me something I can send." He ships work he wouldn't have signed six months ago because the deadline doesn't leave room for the back-and-forth that productive collaboration requires.

I get it. Every cycle strips away a little more of the person's confidence that a productive middle ground exists. It does exist. They haven't been shown how to find it.

*

Step back further. Three credible approaches, working three different mechanisms, and the gap between potential and realized value persists through all of them.

Training changes knowledge without changing the assumptions about your role. You can understand how a language model works and still default to typing a request and accepting whatever comes back. Prompting changes technique without changing contribution quality. You can master every formatting trick and still bring nothing to the interaction that the tool couldn't generate from a generic request. Change management addresses the organizational process without addressing identity threat. You can execute a flawless rollout and still leave senior professionals feeling that their expertise has been diminished rather than amplified.

Each intervention works at its own layer. Each layer matters. But the pattern that persists across all three, the one that no combination of knowledge, technique, and process management resolves, operates underneath: who the person believes they are in the collaboration, whether they see themselves as the essential contributor or the operator, whether the collaboration engages their expertise or bypasses it, whether they can tell when the tool is helping and when it's making things worse. That's the layer. And the evidence for what happens when it's unaddressed isn't abstract. The real-world consequences of operating at the wrong layer make headlines, and the pattern in the headlines is always the same: capable tools, capable people, nobody actually thinking.

CNET published seventy-seven AI-written financial articles and had to correct more than half. The errors weren't subtle. One article got a compound interest calculation wrong: basic arithmetic, the kind any finance journalist would catch on a careful read. But careful reads require cognitive engagement with the output, and the production process had been designed to minimize exactly that. The editors were checking for tone, formatting, and readability. Nobody with financial expertise was asking the question that matters: is this actually right? The surface solution was elegant. Automate the writing, let editors polish. The depth problem went unaddressed: financial accuracy requires someone with domain knowledge engaging with the substance, not just the surface.

The legal profession's encounter with hallucinated citations is even more revealing. By 2025, approximately 712 legal decisions worldwide involved hallucinated AI content, with 90 percent occurring in that year alone. Lawyers, professionals trained in verification and obligated to check citations, submitted fabricated case references to courts. In one filing, twenty-one of twenty-three quotations were invented. Not paraphrased inaccurately. Invented. Cases that never existed, attributed to real courts, with plausible-sounding docket numbers and holdings.

These lawyers weren't incompetent. Many of them had decades of experience. They knew how to verify a citation. They'd done it thousands of times with human-authored briefs. But the AI output looked right, read right, carried every surface signal of a legitimate citation. The formatting was correct. The legal reasoning was coherent. The holdings aligned with the argument being made. Every quality check that a lawyer's training installs (does this read like a real case? does the reasoning hold? does the citation format look right?) returned a false positive. The fluency trap operated in one of the most verification-intensive professions imaginable, and it won.

If lawyers can't resist it, "just check the output" is not a solution. The intervention has to change the relationship to the output, not just remind people to review it more carefully.

The simplest objection to this diagnosis is quality: maybe training fails because the training is bad, not because it's aimed at the wrong layer. Fair enough. That objection deserves the strongest test case available.

The Wharton-run experiment from Chapter 1 is that test case, and the sharpest demonstration of why training quality alone doesn't explain the pattern. The unrestricted version of the tool was, by every conventional metric, a well-designed intervention: smooth access, a capable model, motivated students. It improved performance 48 percent while it was in hand and left the students 17 percent below their own baseline when it was taken away. The tutor version was the same model with one change: it made the student think before it contributed. Improvement more than doubled, and nothing was lost when the tool was removed.

Same tool, same access, one change in what the tool demanded of the student, and categorically different outcomes. That's not a quality gap. That's a layer gap.

*

So if the fix isn't knowledge, and it isn't technique, and it isn't process management, what is it?

The answer lives at the layer these interventions don't reach: the set of assumptions, beliefs, and psychological dispositions that determine how much of the human's actual capability enters the collaboration. What you believe about your role, rather than what you know about AI or how you format a request or how your organization ran the rollout. Whether you see yourself as the essential contributor or the operator. Whether the collaboration demands more from you or less. Whether you can tell when the tool is helping and when it's producing fluent nonsense that will cost you credibility the moment someone looks closely.

The director of strategy from the top of this chapter has the knowledge. She has the technique. Her organization managed the rollout well. And every morning she types a request, accepts what comes back, and ships work that could have come from anyone with the same subscription. The interventions succeeded. The collaboration didn't change. That gap, the one between what the interventions address and what the collaboration actually requires, is the subject of the rest of this book.

Until that layer is on the table, more training, better prompts, and cleaner rollouts will keep succeeding at their own metrics while the collaboration stays where it is. The next chapter is about what that layer is made of, and why it's psychological.

Notes

1. Fernandes, D., Villa, S., Nicholls, S., Haavisto, O., Buschek, D., Schmidt, A., Kosch, T., Shen, C., & Welsch, R. (2025). "AI makes you smarter but none the wiser: The disconnect between performance and metacognition." *Computers in Human Behavior*, 175, 108779. DOI: 10.1016/j.chb.2025.108779.
2. BambooHR (2025). "Think You Can Spot AI? Think Again: 70% of Workers Get It Wrong." Conducted with Method Research.
3. BCG (June 2025). "AI at Work 2025: Momentum Builds, but Gaps Remain." Third annual global AI at Work survey.
4. BCG (2025). "AI Adoption Puzzle: Why Usage Is Up But Impact Is Not."
5. Mirbabaie, M., Brunker, F., Mollmann Frick, N.R.J., & Stieglitz, S. (2022). "The rise of artificial intelligence – understanding the AI identity threat at the workplace." *Electronic Markets*, 32(1), 73-99. DOI: 10.1007/s12525-021-00496-x.
6. Reif, J.A., Larrick, R.P., & Soll, J.B. (2025). "Evidence of a social evaluation penalty for using AI." *Proceedings of the National Academy of Sciences*, 122(19). Four preregistered experiments, N = 4,439.
7. Writer (2026). Enterprise AI adoption report. 79% face AI adoption challenges.
8. Parasuraman, R. & Riley, V. (1997). "Humans and automation: Use, misuse, disuse, abuse." *Human Factors*, 39(2), 230-253. See also: Parasuraman, R. & Wickens, C.D. (2008). "Humans: Still vital after all these years of automation." *Human Factors*, 50(3), 511-520. The motor/mental effort finding is from Cymek, D.H., Truckenbrodt, A., & Onnasch, L. (2023). "Lean back or lean in? Exploring social loafing in human-robot teams." *Frontiers in Robotics and AI*, 10, 1249252. DOI: 10.3389/frobt.2023.1249252.
9. Brehm, J.W. (1966). *A Theory of Psychological Reactance*. Academic Press.
10. CNET (2023). 77 AI-generated financial articles published; over half required corrections.
11. Hallucinated legal citations. Multiple court records and legal reporting, 2023-2025. Approximately 712 legal decisions involving hallucinated AI content.
12. Bastani, H., Bastani, O., Sungu, A., Ge, H., Kabakci, O., & Mariman, R. (2025). "Generative AI without guardrails can harm learning: Evidence

from high school mathematics." *Proceedings of the National Academy of Sciences*, 122(26), e2422633122.

CHAPTER 3

The Layer That Matters

Seventy clinicians walk into a diagnostic study. Not students. Not trainees. Physicians with years of practice, the kind of people whose professional identity is built around a single claim: I know how to diagnose.

The researchers gave them an AI diagnostic tool. But they didn't just hand it over. They built a system that required each clinician to render an independent assessment before seeing the AI's output. Diagnose first. Then look. Then synthesize.

That sequencing matters more than it sounds. Because what the researchers changed wasn't the clinicians' knowledge, or their access to information, or their technical skill with the tool. They changed the order in which expertise met AI output. And that changed the mental model of the collaboration from "check what the machine says" to "bring what you know, then compare."

Diagnostic accuracy improved, against clinicians working with conventional resources.

The AI hadn't gotten better and the clinicians hadn't learned anything new. The structure had installed a different understanding of the human's role. The clinicians were comparing their judgment to a second opinion rather than checking the machine's work, and that distinction, which sounds semantic, is the difference between a human who defers and a human who contributes.

Notice what kind of task this is. Diagnosis is a decision task: the category where Chapter 1's meta-analysis found the steepest losses when humans and AI combined. This study is one exception, and it's instructive about the rule: structure the human's role correctly and even the hardest category can move.

The Wharton study from Chapter 1 showed the same pattern in a different setting: students given unrestricted ChatGPT copied answers and lost everything when the tool was removed. Students given a scaffolded version that asked questions back maintained their gains entirely. Same tool. Same students. The variable was the cognitive structure, the assumption about what the collaboration was for.

In Chapter 2, that study helped explain why training and technique fail. Here, it names what those interventions were missing: the model the person carries about who they are in the collaboration and what the tool is for. Cognitive scientists call it a mental model. And it sits at the layer where every other intervention runs out of reach.

*

The concept isn't new. Philip Johnson-Laird formalized mental models in 1983 as the cognitive representations people construct to reason about situations. They're not accurate maps of reality. They're working models, built from experience, shaped by context, and resistant to revision. When you sit down with a tool, you don't interact with the tool as it is. You interact with your model of the tool, your model of yourself in relation to it, and the assumptions you carry about what should happen when the two meet.

Dedre Gentner and Albert Stevens, working in the same period, showed that people's mental models of technical systems predicted their interaction behavior more reliably than their declarative knowledge about those systems. You can know the right way to use a system and still use it wrong — because your model of the system generates different behavior than your knowledge about the system would prescribe. Knowledge lives in one layer. Behavior lives in another. The mental model is the operating system that sits between them.

Peter Senge brought the idea into organizational thinking in *The Fifth Discipline*, arguing that the assumptions leaders carry about how their organizations work shape every decision they make, usually without their awareness. The mental model operates beneath the surface of conscious choice. It determines which decisions feel available before you ever consciously decide.

Apply this to AI. When someone sits down with a generative AI tool, they carry a mental model of the interaction, whether they've articulated it or not. That model includes assumptions about what the tool can do, what they're supposed to do, whether the tool's output needs their judgment or just their formatting, and what happens to their professional standing if they rely on it.

Here's the thing about operating systems: you can install any application you want, but if the OS is wrong, every application runs badly. Training is an application. Prompt engineering is an application. Change management is an application. The mental model is the operating system underneath all of them. Most AI interventions are installing apps on a broken OS.

The Wharton-run experiment is the clearest demonstration. Both conditions gave students the same application: access to ChatGPT for practice problems. In the unscaffolded condition, the operating system was "AI gives me answers," and the application ran as expected on that OS: type, receive, stop thinking. In the scaffolded condition, the operating system was "AI helps me think," and the same application produced categorically different behavior: engagement, pushback, reasoning before accepting. Chapters 1 and 2 walked the numbers. The point they make here is sharper: no additional training happened between the two conditions, no better prompting technique, no change management framework. The only thing that changed was the mental model of what the collaboration was for. The behavior followed the model.

A cross-country study led by Gerlich reinforced the pattern. With 150 participants across national boundaries, unguided AI use fostered cognitive offloading: participants used the tool as a replacement for thinking rather than an augmentation of it. Structured prompting, which changed the assumed role of the human in the interaction, reduced offloading and enhanced critical reasoning. Same tool. Same general population. Different mental model of the human's job. Different cognitive outcomes.

The mechanism isn't mysterious. When your operating system says "the tool does the work," you behave accordingly: minimal input, uncritical acceptance, cognitive disengagement. When your operating system says "you do the thinking and the tool extends your reach," you behave accordingly: richer input, active evaluation, cognitive engagement. The behavior is rational given the model. The model is the problem.

Think about someone you know who uses AI every day. Maybe it's you. The question to ask isn't whether they've been trained, whether they have access, or whether their organization supports AI adoption. The question is: what do they believe the collaboration is? If they believe it's a delegation relationship, they'll delegate. If they believe it's an amplification relationship, they'll bring what they know into the interaction and expect the output to be better for it. Both beliefs produce coherent behavior. Only one produces valuable outcomes.

This is what Chapters 1 and 2 were circling. The gap between potential and performance. The failure of training, technique, and process management to close it. The 39-percentage-point perception gap. The dependency without capability. All of it traces to the same source: the operating system is wrong, and every intervention aimed at the application layer leaves the OS untouched.

That diagnosis has a practical consequence. If you want durable behavior change in AI collaboration — the kind that transfers across tools, survives model updates, and scales without constant reinforcement — you have to change the operating system: the assumptions, beliefs, and cognitive structures that determine how much of the human's actual capability enters the collaboration. The curriculum, the templates, and the adoption metrics all sit on top of that.

Training changes knowledge. Incentives change motivation. Environmental design changes defaults. All of those produce real changes. But for the class of work this book addresses, high-judgment collaboration where the human must bring genuine expertise, push back on AI, and maintain cognitive engagement, the most durable path runs through the mental model. You can't nudge someone into contributing their scarce input. You can't environmentally design someone out of identity threat. Those require a different operating system.

*

If mental models are the operating system, then the discipline for understanding them is psychology, before computer science, management theory, or information systems get a turn.

That claim needs some care. Both matter. Claude is better than GPT-2. That's technology. Better interfaces, better model capabilities, better integration with workflows: all technology contributions that improved the tools people use. The argument isn't that technology is irrelevant. The argument is about where the binding constraint is now.

The technology works. That was established in Chapter 1. The tools are capable. Most organizations have deployed them. Adoption, by most metrics, is happening. The remaining gap, the one between "using AI" and "getting value from AI," is a gap in how humans relate to the technology. That gap is psychological.

Evidence from more than one direction points the same way. In 2025, Hermann, Puntoni, and Morewedge published a framework in *Trends in Cognitive Sciences* arguing that generative AI threatens workers' basic psychological needs: their needs for competence, autonomy, and relatedness, the three foundations of Self-Determination Theory that Edward Deci and Richard Ryan spent decades establishing as the conditions for sustained human motivation. Their jobs and their access to tools may be fine; the needs take the hit.

The competence need: the experience of being capable, of having skills that matter. When AI produces work comparable to yours in seconds, the felt sense of competence takes a hit, regardless of whether your actual competence has changed.

The autonomy need: the experience of choosing, of directing your own work. When AI generates options faster than you can evaluate them, the locus of decision shifts. You're no longer the author of the strategy. You're the editor of the machine's draft. That's a different psychological experience, even when the output is better.

The relatedness need: the experience of meaningful connection, of your contribution being recognized as yours. When AI mediates the work, the line between "what I produced" and "what the tool produced" blurs. Your colleagues may wonder. You may wonder. That ambiguity erodes the felt sense that your work represents you.

Hermann and colleagues identified five coping strategies people use when AI threatens these needs: direct resolution, symbolic self-completion, dissociation, escapism, and fluid compensation. Some of those strategies are productive. Most aren't. But all of them are psychological responses to a psychological threat, not technical responses to a technical problem.

When *Trends in Cognitive Sciences*, one of the most rigorous cognitive science journals in the field, publishes a framework arguing that the core challenge of AI is fundamentally about psychological needs, the conversation has shifted. The field is converging on the same insight: the binding constraint is psychological.

Which raises an obvious question: hasn't someone said this before? Yes. Emphatically yes.

Trist and Bamforth demonstrated in 1951, in the coal mines of post-war England, that technical systems and social systems must be designed together. Rip out the social structure that made the old technology work, install new technology without accounting for the human system around it, and performance collapses regardless of how good the new equipment is. Seventy-five years of sociotechnical systems theory has built on that foundation.

Plenty of people have worked at the human-technology interface. What's lopsided, for AI specifically, is the investment: billions into tools, infrastructure, and deployment, and far less into understanding why the people using those tools produce mediocre outcomes with them.

The major adoption frameworks tell a precise version of the same story. Davis's Technology Acceptance Model (1989) and Venkatesh's Unified Theory of Acceptance and Use of Technology (2003) predict adoption well: perceived usefulness, ease of use, social influence, facilitating conditions, all psychologically informed. Neither predicts what happens after adoption.

Picture a company that scores perfectly on every TAM factor: the team finds the tool valuable, the interface is intuitive, leadership models AI use visibly, training is available, support is responsive. Adoption hits 90 percent. By every metric in the adoption literature, this is a success story.

Then you pull the output. The proposals are competent and interchangeable. The analyses are technically correct and strategically empty. The deliverables could have come from any team at any firm with the same subscription. Adoption succeeded. Collaboration quality didn't change. The entire measurement apparatus told the organization everything was working. The output told a different story.

TAM was designed to answer "will they pick up the tool?" not "once they're using it, how much of their capability enters the collaboration?" Those are different questions with different answers. The first has decades of studies behind it. The second has far fewer.

The gap psychology addresses comes after all of that: after adoption, after acceptance, after the satisfaction survey. It's the quality of the cognitive and psychological engagement between a human and an AI system, and the conditions under which that engagement produces outcomes neither could produce alone.

Deci and Ryan's Self-Determination Theory provides the theoretical bridge. When AI threatens competence, autonomy, and relatedness, the human response is predictable: withdrawal, deference, resistance, or some combination that degrades the collaboration. The mechanism is psychological need-threat, and SDT explains why capable, trained, willing professionals still produce mediocre outcomes with AI: the tool threatens something more fundamental than their skill set. It threatens their felt sense of agency, competence, and professional meaning.

The meta-analysis from Chapter 1 leaves room for this reading without requiring it. Within each of its 106 experiments the tool was held constant, and the outcomes still split, along task type and along who was stronger going in. If technology were the binding constraint, holding the tool constant would have flattened the variance. It didn't. What the paper measured is that the split exists; the psychology lens is one account of what's driving it, and the rest of this book makes the case.

*

If the problem is psychological, then the most common response to AI, resistance, deserves a second look. Because resistance is usually diagnosed as the problem to solve. People resist change. People resist technology. People resist progress. The organizational response is predictable: communicate benefits, provide training, demonstrate ROI, manage the transition. Overcome the resistance. But what if the resistance isn't a deficiency? What if it's a signal?

Consider the faculty study published in *Frontiers in Communication* in 2025. Researchers found that over a third of university faculty had opted out of generative AI entirely. Not reduced their use. Opted out. The reasons clustered around five themes, and one stood out: "identity in tension."

These aren't technophobes. They're knowledge workers whose professional identity is constructed around the activities AI can now perform: reading critically, writing precisely, evaluating evidence, interpreting meaning. When a machine produces a passable version of the work that defines you, the question isn't "can I use this tool?" The question is "what am I if this tool can do what I do?" That question doesn't have a technical answer.

Their resistance is a coherent response to a genuine threat: a threat to their sense of professional self, to the identity they built over decades of becoming the person who reads, writes, thinks, and judges at a level that matters. Dismissing that resistance as stubbornness or technophobia closes the door to understanding it. And understanding it is the only way through.

Mirbabaie and colleagues established this empirically in 2022, identifying AI-related identity threat as an independent adoption barrier. Independent means it operates on its own channel, separate from knowledge gaps, from change resistance, and from the standard factors adoption models measure. You can close every other gap and identity threat still blocks productive engagement. An organization can train perfectly, deploy thoughtfully, communicate benefits clearly, and still watch a third of its professionals disengage, because no one addressed the question underneath: what is my role now?

The competence penalty research makes the resistance even more rational. Chapter 2 put the numbers on it: a measured competence penalty for using AI, steepest when male non-adopters evaluated female engineers who used the tool: 26 percent. Those are career consequences, not abstractions: a quarter of your perceived competence, gone, for using a tool your organization told you to use, judged by colleagues who chose not to use it themselves. Training programs don't address that, and change management frameworks rarely account for it. The resistance those numbers produce is rational.

Not all resistance is rational, of course. Some is conspiracy theory. Some is generalized technophobia disconnected from any specific threat. Some is plain inertia. The claim isn't that every instance of AI resistance reflects sophisticated identity protection. The claim is that the most common, most consequential, and most systematically misdiagnosed form of resistance, the kind where competent professionals disengage from tools they understand, has rational identity-protective roots. And calling it irrational closes exactly the door you need to open.

Surrender produces the same outcome from the other direction. Surrender and resistance are two faces of the same inadequate mental model. When the model says "this tool threatens what I am," some people protect themselves by rejecting the tool outright. Others protect themselves by capitulating entirely, handing everything over so they don't have to confront what the tool does to their sense of competence. Both responses are rational given the same bad model. Both produce a collaboration where the human's actual capability never enters.

The distinction between resistance and healthy skepticism matters here too. A senior attorney who refuses to let AI draft legal briefs because he's seen it fabricate citations is exercising calibration: rational skepticism based on evidence, which Chapter 1 took care to separate from fight. The faculty member who won't use AI because "machines can't understand literature" is closer to fight mode: protecting an identity claim rather than evaluating a tool. Both look like resistance from the outside. They require different responses.

There's a historical parallel worth holding briefly. In 1984, Craig Brod coined the term "technostress" to describe workers who couldn't cope with the introduction of computers. His contribution was naming the response pattern as a feature of the transition:

workers without the psychological infrastructure for the new technology produced anxiety, frustration, and disempowerment as predictable responses to a situation nobody had prepared them for.

The pattern repeats. But the target has shifted. Computers disrupted clerical and data-entry work: tasks defined by their mechanical precision. AI disrupts judgment work: tasks defined by the human's expertise, interpretation, and cognitive engagement. The psychological mechanism is the same. The identity stakes are categorically higher. When the machine automates filing, you lose a task. When the machine automates analysis, interpretation, and composition, you lose the activities your professional identity was built around. The technostress of 1984 hit the hands. The AI stress of 2025 hits the self.

Reactance theory, which Jack Brehm introduced in 1966, explains part of the mechanism. When people perceive a threat to their behavioral freedom, they resist. AI mandates trigger reactance not because people are anti-technology but because mandates threaten autonomy, one of Deci and Ryan's three basic needs. The standard organizational response to resistance, mandate harder, creates a cycle: more pressure, more reactance, more resistance, more pressure. The intervention amplifies the symptom it's trying to suppress.

But reactance theory doesn't cover the whole picture. The resistance this chapter describes runs deeper than freedom, into identity. A teacher who resists AI writing tools isn't angry that someone told them to use AI. They're protecting the thing that made them a teacher in the first place: the ability to read student writing and know who wrote it, what they understood, where they struggled. When AI makes that skill ambiguous, the teacher's resistance isn't about autonomy. It's about meaning.

It helps to separate AI anxiety into two dimensions. Anticipatory anxiety, the fear of future disruption, is addressable through economic measures and organizational planning. You worry about your job; the organization offers retraining, redeploys you, demonstrates that AI creates new roles. The worry is real, and the response is available.

Annihilation anxiety is something else entirely: the erosion of identity when the machine performs the activities that define you. The word "annihilation" sounds dramatic. It's precise. Not physical destruction. Identity dissolution. The felt experience of watching your professional self become optional. A journalist who spent twenty years developing a voice, a perspective, a way of seeing stories that readers recognize. AI produces a passable version of that voice in thirty seconds. The journalist's anxiety is about losing what made the job meaningful, not just the job itself. That distinction matters, because no economic measure resolves it. No retraining program addresses it. The threat is to the journalist's sense of being a journalist.

That felt experience is the entry point, and treating it as the obstacle is the mistake. When someone feels that their professional identity is threatened by AI, they're telling you something true about their situation. The threat is real. Their expertise is bound to activities that AI now performs. Dismissing the feeling dismisses the person. And a dismissed person doesn't collaborate. They comply, or they disengage, or they leave. None of those produce the kind of high-quality human-AI collaboration the organization needs.

The intervention, then, is to resolve the threat that produces the resistance. Which means answering the question the resistant person is actually asking, even if they haven't articulated it: "What am I worth when the machine can do what I do?"

That question has a good answer. The clinician study at the top of this chapter is a version of the answer in action. The structured workflow didn't fight the clinicians' expertise or threaten their diagnostic identity. It clarified it: you are the diagnostic authority. AI is the second opinion. Your judgment comes first. That framing resolved the threat by making the human's role explicit and essential, not by persuading clinicians that AI was safe or useful or inevitable.

But the answer doesn't live in the technology layer. It doesn't live in the training layer. It lives in the psychological layer that this entire chapter has been naming: the mental model, the operating system, the assumptions about identity and role and value that determine whether the collaboration produces something worth producing.

*

Here's where the three arguments of this chapter converge.

Mental models are the operating system underneath behavior. Change the model and the behavior follows. Leave the model intact and every intervention aimed at the surface (training, technique, process) reverts to baseline when the pressure lifts.

The binding constraint now sits in psychology rather than technology. The tools work. The humans struggle. And the struggle is psychological: identity, self-efficacy, cognitive engagement, calibration. Decades of sociotechnical systems theory, technology acceptance research, and Self-Determination Theory all point to the same layer. The field has the concepts. The practice drops them.

Resistance, the most visible symptom of the struggle, is rational. It's protecting something real. Professional identity, felt competence, the sense that your contribution matters. You can't train away a threat that operates at the identity level. You can't manage around it. You can only resolve it by addressing the mental model that makes the threat feel unresolvable.

So the question becomes: what does a productive mental model look like?

What assumptions would someone carry, what beliefs about their role, their value, and the nature of the collaboration, that would make resistance unnecessary because the threat had been resolved?

What would have to be true about the way a person understood the collaboration for the operating system to run the applications cleanly?

That's the question Part II answers. The mental model has four conditions. Each one addresses a specific psychological mechanism that Chapter 3 has named. Each one resolves a specific form of the struggle that Chapters 1 and 2 documented. Together, they compose the operating system that makes everything else work.

Before the lens shifts, mark where three chapters have landed. The gap is real and measured: combinations that subtract value on average, professionals who can't feel the difference, capability quietly eroding under fluent output. The standard fixes succeed at their own metrics and leave the gap intact, because they work at the application layer. And the layer underneath them is psychological: a mental model of who you are in the collaboration, threatened where identity lives, defended rationally by surrender and by fight. Everything from here builds on that foundation.

The adoption models stop at the door. The automation research named what happens after. What it didn't say is why one person surrenders and the next one fights, and the answer this book gives is a mental model with four conditions in it. Chapter 4 names the model. The four chapters after it take the conditions one at a time.

Notes

1. Everett, S.S., et al. (2026). "From tool to teammate in a randomized controlled trial of clinician-AI collaborative workflows for diagnosis." *npj Digital Medicine*, 9, 409. DOI: 10.1038/s41746-026-02545-1. 70 clinicians, structured assessment protocol.
2. Bastani, H., Bastani, O., Sungu, A., Ge, H., Kabakci, O., & Mariman, R. (2025). "Generative AI without guardrails can harm learning: Evidence from high school mathematics." *Proceedings of the National Academy of Sciences*, 122(26), e2422633122.
3. Johnson-Laird, P.N. (1983). *Mental Models: Towards a Cognitive Science of Language, Inference, and Consciousness*. Harvard University Press.
4. Gentner, D. & Stevens, A.L. (Eds.) (1983). *Mental Models*. Lawrence Erlbaum Associates.
5. Senge, P. (1990). *The Fifth Discipline: The Art and Practice of the Learning Organization*. Doubleday.
6. Gerlich, M. (2025). "From Offloading to Engagement: An Experimental Study on Structured Prompting and Critical Reasoning with Generative AI." *Data* (MDPI), 10(11), 172. DOI: 10.3390/data10110172. N = 150 participants (Germany, Switzerland, UK).

7. Hermann, E., Puntoni, S., & Morewedge, C.K. (2025). "GenAI and the psychology of work." *Trends in Cognitive Sciences*, 29(9). DOI: 10.1016/j.tics.2025.04.009.

8. Deci, E.L. & Ryan, R.M. (1985). *Intrinsic Motivation and Self-Determination in Human Behavior*. Plenum Press. See also: Ryan, R.M. & Deci, E.L. (2000). "Self-Determination Theory and the facilitation of intrinsic motivation, social development, and well-being." *American Psychologist*, 55(1), 68-78.

9. Trist, E.L. & Bamforth, K.W. (1951). "Some social and psychological consequences of the longwall method of coal-getting." *Human Relations*, 4(1), 3-38.

10. Davis, F.D. (1989). "Perceived usefulness, perceived ease of use, and user acceptance of information technology." *MIS Quarterly*, 13(3), 319-340.

11. Venkatesh, V., Morris, M.G., Davis, G.B., & Davis, F.D. (2003). "User acceptance of information technology: Toward a unified view." *MIS Quarterly*, 27(3), 425-478.

12. Vaccaro, M., Almaatouq, A., & Malone, T. (2024). "When combinations of humans and AI are useful: A systematic review and meta-analysis." *Nature Human Behaviour*, 8(12), 2293-2303. 106 experimental studies, 370 effect sizes.

13. Shata, A. (2025). "'Opting out of AI': Exploring Perceptions, Reasons, and Concerns Behind Faculty Resistance to Generative AI." *Frontiers in Communication*, 10, 1614804. DOI: 10.3389/fcomm.2025.1614804. 294 faculty surveyed. Over one-third opted out entirely.

14. Mirbabaie, M., Brunker, F., Mollmann Frick, N.R.J., & Stieglitz, S. (2022). "The rise of artificial intelligence – understanding the AI identity threat at the workplace." *Electronic Markets*, 32(1), 73-99. DOI: 10.1007/s12525-021-00496-x. Three central predictors: changes to work, loss of status/position, and AI identity.

15. Reif, J.A., Larrick, R.P., & Soll, J.B. (2025). "Evidence of a social evaluation penalty for using AI." *Proceedings of the National Academy of Sciences*, 122(19). Four preregistered experiments, N = 4,439.

16. Brod, C. (1984). *Technostress: The Human Cost of the Computer Revolution*. Addison-Wesley.

17. Brehm, J.W. (1966). *A Theory of Psychological Reactance*. Academic Press.

PART II

The Theory

CHAPTER 4

H(x)AI

Two architects open the same AI design tool on the same Monday morning. Both have twenty years of experience. Both are working on office buildings for clients in the same city. Both type their first request before their coffee cools.

The first architect types: "Design a modern four-story office building, 40,000 square feet, with an open floor plan and lots of natural light."

The second architect types something different. She starts with the site: a narrow lot on the east side of downtown, flanked by a 1920s brick warehouse that the city's historic commission won't let anyone touch. She describes the client: a law firm that's been in the same building for thirty years, partners who care about presence but associates who need collaborative space, a managing partner who told her last week that the building should feel like it's been there forever but work like it was built tomorrow. She specifies the constraint that matters most: the western exposure gets brutal afternoon sun, and the partners' offices face west because that's where the view is. The building has to manage solar gain without sacrificing the view that's half the reason the firm is moving.

Both get results in seconds.

The first architect gets a competent modern office building. Glass curtain wall, open floor plan, rooftop terrace. It could be built on any lot in any city for any client. It's the architectural equivalent of "premium sound meets everyday value." Professional. Generic. Forgettable.

The second architect gets something she couldn't have produced alone. The AI proposes a facade system she hadn't considered: perforated metal screens on the western face that reference the brick patterns of the neighboring warehouse, filtering afternoon light into the partners' offices without blocking the skyline. The massing steps back from the historic building in a way that satisfies the commission's setback requirements while creating a terrace on the third floor that the associates will actually use. It's not perfect. She'll spend the next three hours pushing back on the structural assumptions and reworking the lobby circulation. But the starting point is alive because she put something alive into it.

Same tools. Same experience. Same profession. The difference isn't talent, and it isn't the AI. The difference is what happened between them.

*

That difference has a name. And naming it changes how you see every AI interaction you've ever had.

The first three chapters of this book documented a problem: most people get almost nothing from AI while a few get everything. The meta-analysis found human-AI combinations losing to the best of either alone on average, with gains concentrated where the human had real capability to bring. Developers in early 2025 misjudged their own speed with AI by roughly forty points. In one study, knowing more about AI went with judging your own AI-assisted work worse. The interventions on offer address real friction. The argument of this chapter is that the friction isn't where the value goes missing.

This chapter names the place where it does.

The model is called H(x)AI. Written as an equation, formally and exactly once:

Outcome = H(x)AI.

Read the name in order, because it's doing work. H: the human. x: the space between. AI: the artificial intelligence. Three parts, and the middle one is the claim. x isn't a property of the human, and it isn't a property of the tool. It's a property of the space between them: the coupling that decides how much of the human's capability enters the collaboration, and how much of the AI's capability the human draws out. The name puts x exactly where the variable lives: between the two intelligences, touching both. It's the thing that explains why two architects with the same tools and the same experience produce categorically different work.

Be clear about what kind of thing this is before going further, because the shape of an equation promises something the model doesn't deliver. This is not a formula you can plug numbers into. It belongs to the family that includes Maslow's hierarchy, Vroom's expectancy theory, Dweck's mindsets, Lewin's B = f(P, E): models for seeing, not instruments for calculating. You cannot measure H, x, and AI independently and multiply them, and nothing in this book will pretend you can. What the model does is make a previously invisible mechanism visible. And it changes everything about where you look when AI collaboration isn't working.

*

The equation has three components, and the first two are straightforward.

H is human capability: the expertise, judgment, domain knowledge, contextual understanding, and professional experience that the person brings to the table. The second architect has it. So does the first. Twenty years of designing buildings, understanding clients, solving spatial problems. H isn't the differentiator here.

AI is AI capability: the processing power, knowledge base, generative capacity, and speed that the tool provides. Both architects have access to the same model, so AI alone doesn't explain the gap.

x is the variable that governs the coupling. It's the mental model: the set of assumptions, beliefs, and psychological dispositions that determine how much of the human's capability enters the collaboration, and how much of the AI's capability the human draws out. The term has a lineage. Cognitive scientists have used "mental model" since the early 1980s for the working picture a person carries of how something operates, and Peter Senge brought it into management a decade later as the deep assumptions that shape how people act without their noticing. This book uses it in that sense, aimed at one relationship: the picture you carry of what you are for when you sit down with a tool that can do parts of your job. Because of what that picture does in the equation, this book calls it the mental model multiplier. The multiplier, for short.

Watch it run in both directions through the two architects. The first architect withheld everything that made her an architect. The withholding wasn't deliberate or lazy; her mental model of the collaboration didn't include her expertise as an input. She typed a request that anyone could have typed, and she got the tool's generic floor: the output it produces when nothing specific reaches it. Her x was low. Not zero (no one's is), but low enough that the product collapsed.

The second architect's expertise flowed in: the site constraints, the client dynamics, the solar problem, the commission's requirements, the managing partner's contradictory brief. And here's the part a one-way reading misses. What came back was more than her input dressed in the tool's defaults. The perforated-screen facade wasn't in her head, and it wasn't in the tool's generic repertoire either. It surfaced because what she brought gave the AI something real to work against. A high multiplier doesn't just let human capability in. It draws AI capability out. The space between the two is where the collaboration became more than the sum of what either walked in with. Same H. Same AI. A different coupling. A categorically different outcome.

That's the model. Three components, and most of the improvement effort is aimed at two of them. The AI industry optimizes AI. The training industry works on H. The space between them gets less attention, and it's worth being precise about how much less, because this book didn't discover that space and shouldn't pretend to.

The adoption research got there first. TAM, UTAUT, the Technology Readiness Index: decades of validated models that predict, with real accuracy, whether a person will pick up a new tool. They answer the question *will you use it?* Sociotechnical systems research is older still; when Trist and Bamforth studied British coal miners in 1951 they showed that a new technology and the social system around it have to be designed together or the technology underperforms, a finding every failed enterprise rollout re-proves. Parasuraman and Riley, in the automation literature, named misuse and disuse in 1997, too much reliance and too little, and documented both degrading performance. And the mechanisms this book leans on all have owners: reactance, the push-back people feel when something threatens their freedom to act, is Brehm's; self-efficacy, the belief that your effort can produce the result, is Bandura's; the competence, autonomy, and relatedness that Hermann, Puntoni, and Morewedge say generative AI threatens are Deci and Ryan's, from self-determination theory. None of that is new here.

What H(x)AI does is ask the next question and offer an answer. The adoption models stop at yes. Parasuraman documented that people misuse and disuse; he didn't say which one a given person lands on. This book asks: once you're using it, how much of you enters? And it argues that identity and self-efficacy often decide the answer, which is a claim the prior work leaves open rather than one it contradicts.

*

The multiplicative form isn't decorative. It's the argument.

If the relationship between human capability, the mental model, and AI were additive, a weak x would merely subtract some value. The collaboration would still produce something. You'd get less than the maximum, but you'd get something proportional to what you put in.

That's not what the evidence looks like. What the evidence looks like is collapse. Capable experts with powerful tools routinely produce near-zero incremental value. Not slightly reduced value. Not "we got 60 percent of what we could have." Something closer to nothing. The consulting firm from Chapter 1, where every post-AI proposal was interchangeable. The 2025 developer telemetry: more tasks, more bugs, no measurable company-level improvement. The Copilot base, as of Microsoft's early-2026 disclosures a small slice of the commercial users who already had the product at hand. Those are stories of potential evaporating, and in each of them the tool did what it was built to do. The human capability and the tool capability never actually combined.

The multiplicative model captures this all-or-nothing quality. When x approaches zero, it doesn't matter how brilliant the human is or how powerful the AI. The product collapses. A securities attorney with twenty years of experience and the most sophisticated legal research AI on the market produces the same output as a first-year associate with the same subscription if neither of them brings their actual expertise into the interaction. The attorney's knowledge of the judge's prior rulings, his sense of which arguments this particular court finds persuasive, his strategic theory of the case: if none of that enters the collaboration, the tool operates on the generic request it received. And a generic request produces generic output, regardless of how much expertise the person requesting it happens to have stored in their head.

Picture that attorney. He attended the vendor's training workshop, learned the interface, follows the recommended workflow: type the research question, review results, incorporate findings. Six months in, his work product hasn't changed. The tool is capable. His expertise is real. The connection between them is weak. He's operating the tool instead of collaborating with it.

Then something shifts. A case comes in where the opposing counsel has a documented pattern of filing late procedural motions to delay discovery. He knows this because he's faced them three times in the past four years. He brings that knowledge into the research session: "I need case law supporting sanctions for repeated dilatory discovery motions, particularly in the Southern District, where Judge Morrison has shown increasing impatience with this tactic in her last six rulings." The research tool, given context it couldn't have generated from a generic query, surfaces precedent he hadn't found in his own manual searches. He pushes back on two of the suggested cases: wrong procedural posture, wrong jurisdiction. Accepts three others and notices a pattern in the rulings that strengthens his sanctions argument beyond what he'd initially planned.

Notice the direction of the gains. His knowledge went in; capability he couldn't reach alone came out. Same H. Same AI. Different x. The output went from competent legal research to strategic legal intelligence he couldn't have produced by himself, The gap between the two isn't incremental. It's categorical.

Notice, too, how you'd know. Not from the output. The temptation with a model like this is to look at a good result and say "high x," look at a bad one and say "low x," and call that an explanation. That is the result described twice. If x means anything, it has to show up before the outcome does, in things you could check without knowing how the work turned out. Did the attorney put context into the session that wasn't public, that the tool couldn't have had? Did he have a view of the case before he opened the tool, so that he had something to compare its answer against? Did he revise or reject something specific, the two cases with the wrong posture, rather than accept or dismiss the whole? Has he ever gone back to a task he once decided the tool was bad at and tried it again? Those are the marks. When a chapter of this book says someone's x is high, that's the evidence it means, and when it can't point to any of it, it should say "good outcome" and stop there.

*

The multiplicative model didn't appear from nowhere. It has a structural precedent that's been argued over for sixty years.

In 1964, Victor Vroom published *Work and Motivation*, introducing what became Expectancy Theory. His model of motivation uses the same mathematical form: Motivation equals Valence times Instrumentality times Expectancy. How much you want the outcome, multiplied by how strongly you believe effort leads to performance, multiplied by how strongly you believe performance leads to the outcome. If any of the three components is zero, motivation is zero. Not reduced. Zero. A highly valued outcome with no perceived connection between effort and performance produces no motivation at all, no matter how desirable the reward.

Vroom's insight was that motivation is a product of interdependent factors rather than a single quantity you can boost by pulling one lever, and the weakest factor dominates the system. That insight has survived six decades of testing, argument, and extension. H(x)AI borrows the structure and points it at a different question. Vroom's dependent variable is the motivation to act. This book's is the quality of what a human and a machine produce together. The borrowing is of form, not findings; nothing Vroom demonstrated about effort and reward transfers as evidence for this model. What transfers is the logic of the multiplication: you can't compensate for a zero in one term by raising another. Offer someone a million dollars for a task they believe effort can't affect, and motivation stays at zero. Upgrade the model, speed the interface, and it still doesn't matter if the human's capability isn't entering the collaboration. A more capable human doesn't help either, if the mental model keeps the capability out. The weakest term dominates.

So let me be direct about what this model is and what it isn't. H(x)AI is a conceptual framework, not a testable equation. You can't independently measure H, x, and AI, plug in the numbers, and compute a predicted outcome. The components don't have units. The relationship can't be graphed with precision. A researcher looking for falsifiable predictions will find the equation insufficient. And that's fine. Because the most influential models in psychology share exactly this property.

In 1936, Kurt Lewin gave psychology its most famous equation: B = f(P, E). Behavior is a function of the person and the environment. Nobody has ever plugged numbers into it. P and E have no units. It reoriented the field anyway, pulling psychology away from explaining behavior through fixed traits and toward the interaction between people and their situations. H(x)AI descends from the same tradition. B = f(P, E) says behavior emerges from person and situation together; H(x)AI says the value of the collaboration emerges from the human, the mental model, and the tool together, with the mental model standing between the other two, deciding how much of each reaches the other. Maslow's hierarchy of needs is not a testable formula either. You can't calculate a person's self-actualization score from their safety and belonging inputs. Dweck's growth mindset framework has generated legitimate empirical debate about effect sizes and replication. None of these models survive as precise measurement instruments.

All of them changed how millions of people see themselves and their situations. That's their value. Not predictive precision, but perceptual reframing. Lewin gave psychologists a way to stop asking what kind of person does this and start asking what situation produces this. Maslow gave people a way to understand why they couldn't focus on meaning when their rent was due. Dweck gave educators a lens for understanding why some students persisted and others quit.

H(x)AI gives people a way to see why their AI collaboration isn't working and where to intervene. The equation makes the invisible mechanism visible: the variable between the human and the tool that determines whether their capabilities combine or cancel. Its value is in how it changes thinking, not in its mathematical precision.

A reasonable objection here: if the equation isn't testable, why use the equation form at all? Why not just say "your mental model matters"?

Because "your mental model matters" is advice, and advice doesn't change behavior. People nod and keep doing what they were doing. The equation changes how you see the problem. When you understand that the relationship is multiplicative, that a weak x collapses the entire product regardless of how capable you are or how good the tool is, you stop looking at the tool for the answer. You stop looking at training for the answer. You start looking at the one variable that's actually under your control: the quality of the connection between what you know and what the tool can do. The equation is a device for redirecting attention to the thing that makes the difference.

One boundary, stated once and honestly: everything in this model concerns judgment work: work where expertise differentiates the outcome. For work that's mechanical all the way down, the honest conversation is about transition, and Chapter 7 has that conversation directly.

*

The clearest illustration of the multiplicative form is the case where one term was deliberately set to zero.

In February 2024, Klarna announced that its new AI assistant was handling two-thirds of customer service chats and doing the work of seven hundred full-time agents. The Swedish fintech had paused hiring; the CEO, Sebastian Siemiatkowski, talked openly about a smaller company run on AI. Resolution times fell. Cost per interaction fell. By every efficiency metric on the announcement, the bet was paying off.

Fifteen months later, in a May 2025 interview with Bloomberg, Siemiatkowski said what the efficiency metrics hadn't. "As cost unfortunately seems to have been a too predominant evaluation factor when organizing this," he said, "what you end up having is lower quality." Klarna had started recruiting people for customer service again. Investing in the quality of human support, he said, was "the way of the future for us," and it was "so critical" that customers know "there will always be a human if you want."

That's the whole record, and it's enough. Klarna didn't reverse its AI strategy; the assistant kept handling volume, and the company said so. What it reversed was the idea that the human term could go to zero without the product going with it. Read the CEO's own words: cost had been the evaluation factor, and quality was what got evaluated out.

In the language of the model: remove the human entirely and H goes to zero, which takes everything with it. Zero times anything is zero, and it doesn't matter how capable the AI is. A note on the equation's boundaries belongs here. x lives strictly between zero and one: no person who shows up engages at nothing, and nobody's mental model is perfect. But H can leave the equation entirely, because H goes to zero when there is no human in the loop at all. That's what Klarna did for the interactions it automated. It didn't lower the coupling. It removed the space where the coupling happens. There was no between left.

Be careful what this case is evidence for. It says nothing about the four conditions this chapter is about to introduce; no one measured anyone's mental model at Klarna. What it shows is narrower and useful: an organization optimized one term of a multiplicative relationship, treated cost per interaction as if it measured the collaboration, and got what a multiplicative relationship predicts when a term hits zero. Fast, cheap, and, by the CEO's own account, lower quality.

The Klarna story isn't an argument against automation. Some tasks don't require human judgment, and automating them makes sense;

the assistant is still working at Klarna. The story is an argument about category errors: treating a multiplicative relationship as if one factor could substitute for another. Customer service that involves emotional context, regulatory judgment, and discretionary decisions requires all three components. Removing H doesn't simplify the equation. It zeroes it out.

The interesting counterpoint comes from research that seems, at first, to contradict the model.

Erik Brynjolfsson and colleagues studied 5,179 customer support agents at a company that deployed AI assistance. The average productivity improvement was 14 percent. The finding that made headlines lived inside that average: novice workers improved 34 percent. Experienced agents saw minimal impact.

That sounds like it undermines the "human is the scarce input" argument. If novices benefit more, doesn't that mean the AI is the differentiating factor, not the human?

Look closer. The novice agents had low H: limited experience, thin domain knowledge, undeveloped pattern recognition. For them, AI was compensating for capability they hadn't built yet, filling gaps in their knowledge base. The tool was doing the heavy lifting because the human didn't have much to lift. But for experienced agents, H was high. They already knew the product catalog, the common escalation patterns, the regulatory constraints. AI couldn't add much to what they already brought.

Here's where the model earns its keep: the experienced agents weren't necessarily getting less from AI because they needed it less. Some of them, this book would argue, were getting less because they were bringing less of themselves into the interaction. Established routines are harder to adapt. When you've solved a problem the same way for three years, you don't naturally restructure your approach to incorporate a new collaborator. The expertise is there. The willingness to let it interact with the tool's capabilities isn't. High H, low x, minimal impact. The multiplicative model predicts exactly this: capability that doesn't enter the collaboration doesn't contribute to the product. The study didn't measure that, so hold it as a reading, not a result.

There's a second reading of the same data, and it's compatible: AI commoditized the part of the job where experience used to show (the scripted answers, the standard escalations), so some of the experts' old edge relocated rather than vanished. Chapter 7 takes up that thread in full. Both readings end at the same place. The expert advantage that remains is exactly the judgment and contextual knowledge that AI can't replicate, and it becomes more valuable over time, not less. The novice-expert gap will close as the tools improve, because the compensatory benefit for novices shrinks as the baseline rises. What doesn't close on its own is the coupling. The remaining advantage counts only if it enters the collaboration. Only if x is high enough to let it through.

This reframes the entire AI investment conversation. Companies spending millions on better models, faster infrastructure, and more capable tools are optimizing the AI component of a multiplicative equation. That investment pays off only to the extent that human capability is in the product for the upgrade to multiply against. The return on AI investment is gated by a variable the dashboards don't track. Which means the highest-return intervention most organizations could make isn't a technology upgrade. It's helping their people bring more of what they already know into the collaboration they're already having.

*

Here's the part that should change how you think about your own AI collaboration.

Because x multiplies rather than adds, a change in the coupling doesn't show up as a little more of the same. It shows up as a different kind of output. And the difference is starkest at the low end of the range, which is where, by every sign this book can read, most people currently sit.

Consider a financial analyst working near that low end. Nothing about that placement is a measurement; x doesn't come with instrumentation, and this is a picture, not a reading. She uses AI to draft quarterly reports, feeding it the data and accepting the narrative it generates. What she brings is the basic parameters of the client's business, the general market conditions, the standard reporting format. Most of what she knows, the stuff that would make the report genuinely valuable, stays in her head. The client's risk tolerance, which shifted after the board meeting last quarter. The anomaly in receivables that doesn't show up in the summary data but signals a collection problem with their largest customer. The fact that this CFO reads the executive summary and nothing else, so the first paragraph has to carry the strategic argument.

She's getting something from AI. The reports come out faster, the formatting is clean, the boilerplate sections are handled. But the output is interchangeable. Any analyst with the same data and the same subscription would produce the same report.

Now picture her bringing what she knows. She still uses AI for the structure and the boilerplate. But she starts feeding in what only she has. "The receivables aging shows a 12-day extension in the 60-90 bucket, concentrated in three accounts that are all subsidiaries of the same parent company. That's a concentration risk the CFO doesn't know about yet. Frame the receivables section around that finding." She pushes back when the AI's revenue projection doesn't account for the seasonal pattern she's tracked for six quarters. She adds a paragraph on the strategic implication of the margin compression that the AI identified correctly but interpreted through a generic lens instead of through this client's specific competitive position.

She didn't work twice as hard. The AI didn't get better. Much more of what she already knew entered the interaction, and the tool, given something real to work against, started returning analysis she couldn't have pulled from it with a generic request. The other direction of the coupling moved with the first. The report stops being interchangeable. It becomes something only she could have produced, because only she knew this client well enough to make the analysis specific. That is the shape of the return: bringing more of what you already know doesn't improve the output by some proportion. It changes what kind of output it is.

Most people are sitting somewhere in the low range. That placement is an observation from twenty years of watching the pattern, not a measurement; nothing about x can be measured. The capability is there. The mental model, the assumptions about their role in the collaboration and what their contribution is worth, keeps most of the expertise out of the interaction. Moving takes no new training, no new tools, no personality transplant. It takes a shift in how you see your own role: from operator to essential contributor.

I keep coming back to that when I look at the Vaccaro data, the developer studies, the enterprise adoption numbers. Closing the gap between potential and realized value doesn't require genius. It requires the expertise people already have to enter a collaboration it's currently locked out of. The returns on that shift are large precisely because so few people are making it.

And the shift compounds. An analyst who starts feeding her contextual knowledge into AI interactions doesn't just produce better reports. She starts noticing what contextual knowledge she has. The collaboration becomes a mirror: the more she contributes, the more clearly she sees what she knows that the tool doesn't. Three months in, she's not just using AI differently. She understands her own expertise differently. The mechanical parts of her job, the formatting, the data aggregation, the boilerplate language, fall away, and what remains is the judgment, the pattern recognition, the client knowledge that no tool can replicate. That's a professional identity clarification, the subject of Chapter 7.

Nobody reaches the top of the range. Nobody will. The range isn't a target to optimize; it's a lens for understanding where you are and what moving looks like. The practical question is double, because the coupling is: what am I withholding from this interaction that I already know? And what could this tool give me that I'm not asking for? The answer to the first, for most people, is almost everything that makes them valuable. The answer to the second is most of what they bought.

*

So what determines x? What is this mental model made of, and how does it change?

That's the question the next four chapters answer.

x isn't fixed, and it isn't a trait. It's a set of beliefs about yourself, about the tool, and about the nature of the collaboration — beliefs that were formed before AI arrived and that AI's arrival didn't automatically update. The architect who typed the generic request didn't lack curiosity or intelligence. She had a mental model of AI as a production tool: something you instruct, not something you collaborate with. That model was shaped by every previous technology she'd adopted, from CAD software to email, and it told her that the tool does the work while the human manages the tool. The model was wrong, but it was invisible, and invisible models don't get corrected. They get reinforced by every interaction that confirms them. Which means x, left unexamined, tends to stay where it starts.

The model identifies four conditions: four psychological shifts that move x upward. They aren't steps in a sequence. The claim is that they work as a system, each one reinforcing the others, each addressing a specific mechanism that keeps expertise out of the space between. That claim is a hypothesis, and this book will hold it as one. No study has tested all four together. One randomized trial of clinicians, which Chapter 3 told and Chapter 8 returns to, changed a workflow so that doctors committed to their own diagnosis before seeing the model's, and in doing so touched two of the conditions at once, effort and calibration, with better diagnostic accuracy than clinicians working with conventional resources.

That's suggestive. It's one study, in one domain, and it doesn't confirm the system.

The first condition reframes who you are in the relationship: you are the scarce input, the non-commodity factor, the thing that makes the output valuable rather than generic. The second reframes what the collaboration should feel like: harder, not easier, because the effort of bringing your judgment into the interaction is the multiplier in action. The third addresses the identity threat directly: AI doesn't diminish your professional identity, it clarifies it, stripping away the mechanical to reveal what your expertise always actually was. The fourth installs an ongoing practice: calibration, the habit of checking whether your model of AI's capabilities still matches reality. That last one is the AI-facing half of the coupling: the first three govern what you bring, the fourth governs what you're able to draw out, and it keeps the other three honest as the tools change underneath you.

Each condition has its own evidence, its own illustrations, its own chapter. Together, they constitute the intervention that training, prompting, and change management don't reach. Not because those approaches are wrong, but because they operate at the surface while the four conditions operate at the layer that generates the behavior.

The second architect from the top of this chapter wasn't following a checklist. She wasn't using a special prompting technique. She didn't attend a workshop on "AI-enhanced design." She was operating with a mental model that said: my knowledge of this site, this client, and this design problem is what makes this collaboration worth having. The solar gain problem, the historic commission, the managing partner's contradictory brief — she brought all of it because she believed it mattered. That belief, and the behaviors it generated, is what the four conditions describe and what the rest of this book makes available.

The equation is simple. The implications aren't. If x is the variable, and x is a mental model, then improving AI collaboration is a seeing problem before it is a technology problem or a training problem. You have to see yourself differently in the collaboration before the collaboration can produce something different.

And the evidence says most people aren't seeing it yet. The large majority of Microsoft's commercial base that had Copilot at hand in early 2026 and didn't buy it, the developers who believed they were faster when they were slower, the consultants whose post-AI proposals are interchangeable: they're not failing because they lack capability. They're failing because the capability they have doesn't enter the collaboration they're having.

Which means the gap between what AI collaboration could produce and what it currently produces is waiting on the variable in the middle of the name. The next four chapters are about what moves it.

Notes

1. Vaccaro, M., Almaatouq, A., & Malone, T. (2024). "When combinations of humans and AI are useful: A systematic review and meta-analysis." *Nature Human Behaviour*, 8(12), 2293-2303. DOI: 10.1038/s41562-024-02024-1. 106 experiments, 370 effect sizes; significant moderators include task type and the relative performance of human versus AI alone.

2. Becker, J., Rush, N., Barnes, B., & Rein, D. (2025). "Measuring the impact of early-2025 AI on experienced open-source developer productivity." METR, July 10, 2025. arXiv:2507.09089. See also the authors' February 24, 2026 update, https://metr.org/blog/2026-02-24-uplift-update/, which treats the 2025 slowdown as a snapshot of early-2025 tools.

3. Fernandes, D., Villa, S., Nicholls, S., Haavisto, O., Buschek, D., Schmidt, A., Kosch, T., Shen, C., & Welsch, R. (2025). "AI makes you smarter but none the wiser: The disconnect between performance and metacognition." *Computers in Human Behavior*, 175, 108779. DOI: 10.1016/j.chb.2025.108779.

4. Johnson-Laird, P.N. (1983). *Mental Models: Towards a Cognitive Science of Language, Inference, and Consciousness*. Harvard University Press. Gentner, D. & Stevens, A.L. (Eds.). (1983). *Mental Models*. Erlbaum. Senge, P. (1990). *The Fifth Discipline: The Art and Practice of the Learning Organization*. Doubleday.

5. Davis, F.D. (1989). "Perceived usefulness, perceived ease of use, and user acceptance of information technology." *MIS Quarterly*, 13(3), 319-340. Venkatesh, V., Morris, M.G., Davis, G.B., & Davis, F.D. (2003). "User

acceptance of information technology: Toward a unified view." *MIS Quarterly*, 27(3), 425-478. Parasuraman, A. (2000). "Technology Readiness Index (TRI): A multiple-item scale to measure readiness to embrace new technologies." *Journal of Service Research*, 2(4), 307-320. DOI: 10.1177/109467050024001.

6. Trist, E.L. & Bamforth, K.W. (1951). "Some social and psychological consequences of the longwall method of coal-getting." *Human Relations*, 4(1), 3-38.

7. Parasuraman, R. & Riley, V. (1997). "Humans and automation: Use, misuse, disuse, abuse." *Human Factors*, 39(2), 230-253.

8. Brehm, J.W. (1966). *A Theory of Psychological Reactance*. Academic Press.

9. Bandura, A. (1977). "Self-efficacy: Toward a unifying theory of behavioral change." *Psychological Review*, 84(2), 191-215.

10. Deci, E.L. & Ryan, R.M. (1985). *Intrinsic Motivation and Self-Determination in Human Behavior*. Plenum. Ryan, R.M. & Deci, E.L. (2000). "Self-determination theory and the facilitation of intrinsic motivation, social development, and well-being." *American Psychologist*, 55(1), 68-78.

11. Hermann, E., Puntoni, S., & Morewedge, C.K. (2025). "GenAI and the psychology of work." *Trends in Cognitive Sciences*, 29(9). DOI: 10.1016/j.tics.2025.04.009.

12. Faros AI (2025). "The AI Productivity Paradox." 10,000+ developers, 1,255 teams. 21% more tasks, 9% more bugs per developer, no significant company-level improvement.

13. Microsoft earnings disclosures, FY2026 Q2 (January 28, 2026: ~15 million paid Microsoft 365 Copilot seats against a ~450-million commercial base) and FY2026 Q3 (April 29, 2026: "over 20 million" paid seats). Dated snapshots; see Chapter 1, Note 20.

14. Vroom, V.H. (1964). *Work and Motivation*. John Wiley & Sons. Multiplicative model of motivation (valence × instrumentality × expectancy); dependent variable is motivation to act, not collaboration quality.

15. Lewin, K. (1936). *Principles of Topological Psychology*. McGraw-Hill. Source of B = f(P, E): behavior is a function of the person and the environment.

16. Klarna. February 27, 2024 press release: AI assistant handling two-thirds of customer service chats, "doing the equivalent work of 700 full-time agents." Siemiatkowski, S., interview with Bloomberg, May 8, 2025, as reported by CX Dive (May 2025) and Forbes (May 18, 2025): "As cost unfortunately seems to have been a too predominant evaluation factor when organizing this, what you end up having is lower quality"; "Really investing in the quality of the human support is the way of the future for

us"; "there will always be a human if you want." Klarna announced recruitment of human customer-service staff in the same period.

17. Brynjolfsson, E., Li, D., & Raymond, L. (2023). "Generative AI at Work." NBER Working Paper No. 31161; published in *The Quarterly Journal of Economics* (2025). 5,179 customer support agents. 14% average improvement; 34% for novices, minimal for experienced agents.

18. Everett, S.S., Bunning, B.J., Jain, P., Lopez, I., Agarwal, A., Desai, M., Gallo, R., Goh, E., Kadiyala, V.B., Kanjee, Z., Koshy, J.M., Olson, A., Rodman, A., Schulman, K., Strong, E., Chen, J.H., & Horvitz, E. (2026). "From tool to teammate in a randomized controlled trial of clinician-AI collaborative workflows for diagnosis." *npj Digital Medicine*, 9, 409. DOI: 10.1038/s41746-026-02545-1. Cited here only as the one trial whose structured workflow touched two of the four conditions at once.

CHAPTER 5

I Am the Scarce Input

A consultant opens ChatGPT, types "create a Q4 marketing campaign strategy for a premium skincare brand targeting millennials," and gets back something that looks like a strategy. Professional formatting. Reasonable recommendations. Seasonal messaging pillars. A social media calendar with platform-specific content themes. He cleans it up, sends it to the client, and moves on to the next project. Forty-five minutes, start to finish. It feels productive.

A second consultant gets the same brief. He doesn't start with AI. He starts with what he knows: this brand is third in its category, not first. The customers who stay aren't buying for aesthetics; they're buying for ingredient sourcing transparency, a finding from a focus group the client ran six months ago that nobody on the current team has read. Email consistently outperforms social for this brand's buyer demographics, a pattern visible in eighteen months of campaign data sitting in a dashboard nobody checks. And the CEO mentioned in a board meeting that the real priority is moving upmarket, not defending the current position. The consultant types none of this as a prompt. He types all of it as the beginning of a collaboration: here is what I know that you don't. Here is the strategic context that makes generic advice dangerous. Now help me build something that accounts for all of it.

The output he gets back is unrecognizable from the first consultant's. It's specific to this brand's competitive position. It reflects the actual buyer psychology. It addresses the CEO's real priority instead of the brief's stated one. It contains strategic judgment that no competitor with the same AI subscription could replicate, because the judgment came from him.

Same tool. Same subscription. Same Tuesday morning. The variable that separated the two outputs wasn't the AI. It was what the human brought to the table.

*

That difference is the first condition of the H(x)AI framework, and it rests on a structural fact about how human-AI collaboration works: AI is abundant. You are not. Not in the motivational-poster sense, not "you are special and irreplaceable." In the economic sense. The capabilities AI contributes to a collaboration are available to everyone. The capabilities you contribute are available to no one else.

Processing power, broad knowledge, tireless availability, speed: these are AI's contributions, and they're available to everyone. Every competitor. Every peer. Every junior hire with the same subscription. When the input to a collaboration is something AI can generate on its own, the output is commodity. Professional, competent, and indistinguishable from what anyone else would get. The skincare strategy the first consultant produced wasn't bad. It was generic. It was the strategy that any marketer typing the same request into the same tool would receive. Which means it added nothing that the client couldn't have gotten without him.

The second consultant's output was different because he contributed something AI couldn't source: competitive intelligence specific to this brand, customer research nobody else had synthesized, a read on executive priorities that existed in a board meeting, not a database. Those inputs are scarce. They exist in one person's head, built from years of working in this category, this account, this relationship. AI can process them, extend them, challenge them, build on them. AI cannot generate them.

One caveat, stated now because Condition 4 will pick it up: the boundary between what AI can and can't source isn't fixed. Capabilities move quarterly. What stays true is the structure. Whatever the tool can generate on its own is, by that fact, commodity, and the frontier of what only you can supply is something you have to keep locating, not something you get to memorize. Calibration, the fourth condition, is how you track it.

This is the structural argument underneath Condition 1: for work where judgment matters, where context shapes the answer, where expertise is the differentiator, the human is the scarce input. Not because humans are inherently superior to AI. Because in a world where AI capability is universally accessible, the only thing that makes one collaboration's output different from another's is what the human contributed that the tool couldn't have produced alone.

Where that claim applies, and where it doesn't, needs saying once, plainly, and it will be repeated in the next two chapters wherever the claim travels. For judgment work, strategy, diagnosis, creative direction, any decision that turns on context: the human is the scarce input, the effort of bringing that input is what multiplies, and the mechanical layer around it can be handed to the tool without loss. For routine, well-specified execution, ease is the right feeling, the AI may well be the scarce input, and "harder is better" doesn't apply. For work that is mechanical all the way down, the honest word is displacement, and this book won't promise a hidden judgment layer where there isn't one. And for creative craft where the technique is the art, brushwork, sentence rhythm, a coder's style as a signature, the line between mechanical and essential is messy, and it's more honest to say so than to pretend the split is clean.

A study of developers using GitHub Copilot shows one end of that line. Researchers at GitHub and Microsoft gave developers a specific, well-defined task: build a JavaScript HTTP server. Clear requirements, a known solution pattern, minimal judgment required. With Copilot, they finished about 55 percent faster. On that task the AI was doing the heavy lifting; any developer with the same subscription would have gotten roughly the same result. The study measured that one task and nothing else. It says nothing about what happens when the work moves from following a pattern to choosing which pattern to follow, and it would be a misreading to make it say so. What it does is mark the routine end of the line cleanly: here, the AI is the scarce input.

The other end of the line, where judgment decides the outcome and the tool's contribution shrinks or reverses, is where most knowledge workers live. Chapter 8 tells the study that measured it. For now, the point is about where people think they are. Most professional work sits on the judgment side of the line. Most professionals are working as if they're on the routine side.

*

The reason most people don't bring their full expertise into AI collaboration isn't laziness. It isn't ignorance. Time pressure plays a part; so do incentives that reward volume over judgment. But the psychological driver, the one this chapter is about, is more specific and more damaging: they don't believe their contribution matters.

Albert Bandura spent decades establishing that self-efficacy, a person's belief in their ability to produce desired outcomes through their own actions, determines effort and persistence more reliably than actual ability does. People who believe they can succeed try harder, persist longer, and recover faster from setbacks. People who doubt their efficacy withdraw, reduce effort, and interpret ambiguous feedback as confirmation that they were right to doubt themselves. The mechanism is consistent across domains: athletic performance, academic achievement, career development, health behavior. What you believe about your capability shapes what you attempt, which shapes what you achieve, which shapes what you believe. The cycle is self-reinforcing in both directions.

Apply that to AI collaboration and the pattern snaps into focus. When a knowledge worker sits down with a tool that seems to know everything, writes fluently, responds instantly, and never gets tired, the implicit comparison is devastating. The tool appears infinitely capable. The human feels finite. Expertise that took a decade to build, the kind that used to be a career differentiator, now seems redundant when the AI can produce a competent first draft in thirty seconds.

The conclusion people draw, usually without articulating it, is that their contribution doesn't add much. So they contribute less. They type a generic request instead of bringing their specific knowledge. They accept the first output instead of pushing back with their own judgment. They use AI the way you use a vending machine: insert request, receive product. The expertise doesn't disappear. It just never enters the interaction.

And here's the trap: when you withhold your expertise, the output is generic. When the output is generic, it confirms the belief that AI does the real work and you're just along for the ride. The self-efficacy collapse becomes self-fulfilling. You contributed less because you didn't think your contribution mattered. The output was mediocre because your contribution was missing. The mediocre output proved, to you, that your contribution doesn't matter.

This isn't a new pattern. Parasuraman and Wickens documented it in automation research under the term "complacency," extending findings that go back decades in aviation and industrial control. They studied what happens when human operators work alongside automated systems in aviation, industrial control, medical monitoring. The finding was consistent: operators who trust automated systems reduce their monitoring effort, which degrades the joint human-machine performance, which they don't notice because they've stopped monitoring. The complacency loop was a known problem in cockpits and control rooms long before anyone typed a prompt into ChatGPT.

The mechanism in AI collaboration is the same, with an additional twist that makes it worse. In a cockpit, complacency occasionally produces a visible failure: a missed alarm, a deviation from the flight path. The feedback, when it comes, is unambiguous. In AI collaboration, the degradation is invisible. A generic strategy looks professional. A shallow analysis reads smoothly. The quality signals that would normally trigger a "this isn't good enough" response have been neutralized by AI's ability to produce polished mediocrity. The output is fluent, formatted, confident. It just isn't good. And without domain expertise actively evaluating it, nobody notices.

The deference trap, as this book will call it, isn't a character flaw. It's a predictable consequence of a specific psychological state: low self-efficacy in the context of a tool that appears to render your expertise unnecessary. And it operates independently of how much a person actually knows. The most experienced professionals are not immune; sometimes they're the most vulnerable, because they have the most to lose. A partner at a law firm with twenty-five years of trial experience can fall into the same pattern if she begins to believe that AI's legal research capability makes her strategic judgment less essential. A chief product officer who has launched forty products can watch AI generate a product roadmap and quietly wonder whether his instinct for market timing still matters. The expertise is still there. It just stops entering the collaboration.

*

One study caught this happening in real time.

Wu and colleagues, writing in *Scientific Reports*, tested what happens to intrinsic motivation when people move from solo work to AI-assisted work. Same people, same kinds of tasks, solo first, then with AI. The finding was precise and uncomfortable. Collaboration with generative AI enhanced task performance but undermined intrinsic motivation. People working with AI produced better outputs by conventional measures, and they reported sharp declines in perceived control. The sense of being the agent in the interaction, the one making choices and directing the work, eroded when AI entered the picture.

That perceived-control finding is the mechanism that makes the self-efficacy collapse dangerous. It's not just that people feel less confident. They feel less like the work is theirs. The locus of agency shifts from "I am producing this with AI's help" to "AI is producing this and I'm editing." The distinction sounds subtle. It changes everything about what the person brings to the interaction. When you feel like the agent, you contribute your best thinking. When you feel like the editor, you clean up someone else's.

And the drop appeared at the point of transition, the moment AI entered the workflow, rather than accumulating over months. People didn't slowly lose confidence in their contribution. They reassessed it as soon as they were confronted with a tool that could produce polished output without them. It's one study, and it measured motivation rather than the quality of what people contributed. But it lines up with Bandura's prediction exactly: reduced self-efficacy, reduced effort. The disengagement isn't a choice. The psychological conditions for engagement were undermined by the collaboration itself.

This is what makes the AI self-efficacy problem different from garden-variety Dunning-Kruger or general metacognitive bias. Dunning-Kruger describes people who overestimate their ability. The AI collaboration problem describes people who underestimate their relevance. They may know perfectly well how capable they are; the consultant with twenty years of brand strategy experience doesn't suddenly forget she's good at brand strategy. What she's lost is the belief that her capability matters in the presence of the tool. That's an identity gap, and it's the gap Condition 1 is designed to close.

*

Condition 1 doesn't close it by reassuring people. "AI won't replace you" is the reassurance version, and it fails for the same reason all reassurance fails: it addresses the fear without changing the structural understanding that produces the fear. Telling a consultant that AI won't take her job doesn't change the fact that she just watched it produce a strategy in forty-five seconds that would have taken her a day. The reassurance rings hollow because the experience contradicts it.

Condition 1 closes the gap by reframing the structure. The question isn't whether you'll be replaced. The question is what makes one AI-assisted output valuable and another one generic. The answer, visible in the studies this book has told, is the quality of the human contribution. AI produces commodity output when the human brings commodity input. AI produces extraordinary output when the human brings what only they can bring: judgment built from experience, context gathered from relationships, taste developed over a career, knowledge that exists in one person's head because they did the work to put it there.

The reframe is structural, not motivational. It's not "believe in yourself." It's "look at the economics." AI capability is universally accessible. Your domain expertise is not. Your contextual knowledge is not. Your judgment about what matters for this client, this market, this situation is not. In an environment where everyone has access to the same infinitely capable tool, the only variable that differentiates output is what the human contributed. The scarce input is you.

The meta-analysis from Chapter 1 makes the economics visible at scale, and it's worth one more sentence here because of what its moderators say. Across 106 experiments, the combinations that beat the best of either alone were the ones where the human already outperformed the AI on the task, and the gains sat in creation work rather than decision work. Read as economics: where there was real human capability to bring, bringing it paid; where there wasn't, adding a human to the loop cost more than it returned.

Participation isn't the same as contribution. You have to bring something the AI can't source independently. If your input is redundant with what the tool would generate on its own, you're not the scarce input. You're overhead.

This is where the critique of prompt engineering from Chapter 2 finds its resolution, and it's worth being exact about who that critique was aimed at. Chapter 2 argued that prompting as the industry usually teaches it, templates, syntax tricks, "act as" formulas, is a perishable skill aimed at the wrong layer. That argument stands. It was never aimed at the practitioners who already put everything they know into the box: the client's history, the constraint the brief left out, the number they don't trust and why. Those people are doing expert prompting, and expert prompting is Condition 1 by another name. What separates them from the template-followers isn't syntax. It's that they bring something the tool can't source, and that something makes the output unreplicable. H(x)AI doesn't correct what they're doing. It names the mechanism, so that it can be seen and taught rather than admired and imitated.

*

The difference between "using AI" and "contributing to a collaboration" becomes concrete when you watch two people do the same work. Picture them. The mechanics look identical from the outside: both sit at a computer, both type into the same interface, both receive a response. The difference is entirely in what crosses from the person's head into the input field.

A data analyst needs to prepare a quarterly business review for the enterprise segment. Analyst A opens ChatGPT, pastes in the retention data, and types: "Summarize the key trends." Three observations come back, all accurate, all obvious, all things anyone looking at the data would notice. Revenue is flat. Churn increased slightly. New logos are down quarter over quarter. The analyst formats the summary, drops it into a slide deck, and moves on. She concludes that AI isn't particularly useful for real analysis. Too surface-level.

Analyst B opens the same tool with the same data but brings something different into the interaction: "I'm looking at Q1 retention data for our enterprise segment. Last quarter we saw unusual churn in the mid-market tier after the pricing change. I suspect the enterprise segment is showing early warning signs of the same pattern. The three accounts that churned last quarter all had the same profile: post-Series B, under pressure to cut costs, contracted during the growth phase when our pricing was lower. Help me identify whether the leading indicators in the current enterprise cohort match what we saw in mid-market before the churn accelerated."

The output is different in kind. It's specific to this company's pricing history. It's grounded in a hypothesis that only someone who tracked last quarter's churn would have. It surfaces a pattern in the enterprise data that confirms the analyst's suspicion and identifies three accounts showing the same early indicators. The analysis is actionable in a way that "revenue is flat" never could be, because the human's domain knowledge was in the input.

The tool didn't change. The data didn't change. What changed was whether the analyst's expertise entered the collaboration or stayed in her head. Analyst A used AI. Analyst B contributed to a collaboration. The distinction is the entire argument of this chapter. And it's testable with a simple question: if you handed this same prompt to anyone else with the same AI subscription, would the output be meaningfully different? If the answer is no, you haven't brought the scarce input. Call it the commodity test. It isn't abstract. It's a practical diagnostic, and it has the property Chapter 4 asked for: you can run it before you see whether the output was any good. Apply it to the last five things you asked AI to help with. How many of them would have produced the same output regardless of who was asking?

That question tends to land hard. Most people discover that three or four out of five interactions were commodity. The expertise was there. It just didn't enter the interaction. They asked AI to do something generic, got something generic back, and concluded that AI is useful for drafts but not for real thinking. The tool wasn't the problem. The input was.

*

There's a temptation, when presenting a condition like this one, to universalize it: to claim that everyone has scarce expertise and every job has a hidden judgment layer waiting to be activated. That would be comforting. It would also be false, and the scope stated earlier in this chapter is the reason the book won't do it. Some work is mechanical all the way down. A data entry specialist whose job is entirely moving values from one system into another doesn't have hidden expertise to reveal, and for that work AI is displacement, not an invitation to contribute more of yourself. Pretending otherwise is dishonest and patronizing.

What this book addresses is the vast middle: the millions of knowledge workers whose jobs combine mechanical execution with genuine judgment, who have real expertise that would make AI output dramatically better, and who aren't bringing it. The expertise is there. Few of them have been told it's the essential ingredient.

The honest version requires looking at your own work and asking which parts involve genuine judgment and which parts are routine execution that AI can handle without you. Most knowledge workers will find that the ratio is more favorable than they assumed. The judgment component of their work is larger and more valuable than they've been treating it. But the answer has to come from an honest assessment, not from a reassuring framework that tells everyone what they want to hear.

*

Here's what changes when someone internalizes Condition 1.

The shift isn't dramatic from the outside. It doesn't look like a transformation. It looks like someone who types a different kind of first message. Instead of "write me a marketing plan," it's "here's what I know about this market that you don't, and here's the strategic question I'm actually trying to answer." Instead of "summarize this data," it's "here's the hypothesis I'm testing and why I think last quarter's pattern is relevant." The input changes. The output follows.

The deeper shift is internal. The person stops experiencing AI as something that makes their expertise less relevant and starts experiencing it as something that makes their expertise more powerful. That shift, from threat to amplifier, doesn't require new skills or a different subscription. It requires a different understanding of where value comes from.

A financial analyst who brings her knowledge of a client's risk tolerance, the board's unspoken priorities, and last quarter's anomalies into an AI interaction isn't competing with the tool. She's using it to extend what she already knows into territory she couldn't have covered alone. The tool handles the breadth. She provides the depth. The combination produces something neither could have produced independently.

That's the productive mental model Condition 1 installs: you are the scarce input. Not as reassurance. As structural fact. When the tool is universally accessible, the differentiator is what you bring that nobody else can bring. Your expertise. Your context. Your judgment about what matters. The years you spent learning what doesn't work in this category, the relationships that taught you what this client actually needs, the pattern recognition that only comes from doing the work long enough to see the cycles repeat.

AI is powerful; that was never in question. The question is whether your expertise enters the collaboration or sits unused while you accept commodity output. The first condition says: bring it. All of it. Because without it, the most powerful tool in the world produces work that could have come from anyone. And work that could have come from anyone, no matter how polished, is worth exactly what anyone would charge for it.

The next chapter asks what happens when you do bring it, because the answer is counterintuitive: it gets harder. Productive AI collaboration demands more of you, not less. And that turns out to be the point.

Notes

1. Bandura, A. (1977). "Self-efficacy: Toward a unifying theory of behavioral change." *Psychological Review*, 84(2), 191-215.
2. Peng, S., Kalliamvakou, E., Cihon, P., & Demirer, M. (2023). "The Impact of AI on Developer Productivity: Evidence from GitHub Copilot." arXiv:2302.06590. Controlled experiment on a single specified task (a JavaScript HTTP server); developers with Copilot finished ~55% faster. The study did not test architectural or design work; claims about the judgment end of the task spectrum are not drawn from it.
3. Parasuraman, R. & Wickens, C.D. (2008). "Humans: Still vital after all these years of automation." *Human Factors*, 50(3), 511-520. Documented complacency in automation: operators reduce monitoring effort when they trust automated systems. See also: Parasuraman, R. & Riley, V. (1997). "Humans and automation: Use, misuse, disuse, abuse." *Human Factors*, 39(2), 230-253.
4. Wu, S., Liu, Y., Ruan, M., Chen, S., & Xie, X.-Y. (2025). "Human-generative AI collaboration enhances task performance but undermines human's intrinsic motivation." *Scientific Reports*, 15, 15105. DOI: 10.1038/s41598-025-98385-2. Enhanced task performance but undermined intrinsic motivation; sharp declines in perceived control at the transition from solo to AI collaboration. Single experimental study.
5. Vaccaro, M., Almaatouq, A., & Malone, T. (2024). "When combinations of humans and AI are useful: A systematic review and meta-analysis." *Nature Human Behaviour*, 8(12), 2293-2303. DOI: 10.1038/s41562-024-02024-1. Moderators: task type (losses on decision tasks, gains on content creation) and relative baseline (gains when the human alone outperformed the AI alone). See Chapter 1, Note 1.

CHAPTER 6

The Collaboration Demands More of Me, Not Less

A consultant sits down to write a competitive analysis for a client in the industrial packaging market. He's been in this industry for eleven years. He knows the three competitors who actually matter, the two who are noise, and the regulatory shift that's about to scramble pricing for everyone. He opens his AI tool and types: "Write a competitive analysis of the industrial packaging market, focusing on key players, trends, and strategic implications."

Forty-five minutes later, he has a polished document. Professional formatting. Clean prose. Reasonable recommendations about market consolidation and sustainability trends. He reads it, fixes a few phrasings, and sends it to the client. It feels productive.

The next week, different client, same category. This time he tries something different. Before opening the AI tool, he writes his own assessment: the three competitors he's watching, why he thinks the mid-tier player is about to make an acquisition, the regulatory filing he spotted that nobody in the industry is talking about yet, and his read on why the client's current pricing strategy won't survive the next eighteen months. Then he brings that to the collaboration: "Here's my analysis of this market. Challenge it. What am I missing? Where's the data that contradicts my read on the regulatory shift? What competitive dynamics am I underweighting?"

Two hours later, he has something else entirely. The AI surfaced a patent filing he hadn't seen, one that confirmed his acquisition hypothesis from a different angle. It challenged his pricing timeline with data he hadn't considered, and he pushed back on half of it because the data didn't account for the client's contract structure. He incorporated two insights that genuinely changed his thinking and discarded three that sounded plausible but didn't hold up against what he knew about this specific market.

The first draft is competent. Any consultant with the same subscription could have produced it. The second draft is his: specific, strategic, grounded in a decade of pattern recognition that no AI model carries. The time difference isn't the story. The cognitive engagement difference is. The 45-minute version felt productive. The two-hour version was productive.

That distinction is the second condition of productive AI collaboration, and it's the most counterintuitive claim in this book: working well with AI should feel harder, not easier.

*

The dominant narrative about AI is an efficiency story. AI makes work faster, smoother, less effortful. And for routine tasks, that's exactly right. Using AI to format a document, compile a dataset, or draft a standard email should be frictionless. Efficiency is the point. Nobody needs to bring deep professional judgment to a calendar invitation.

The problem is that efficiency feels good regardless of whether it's appropriate. The subjective experience of "this was easy" doesn't carry a label telling you whether you just saved time on a routine task or whether you just skipped the thinking that would have made the output valuable. Both register the same way: as productivity. As getting things done. As the tool working.

But the efficiency narrative has metastasized beyond routine work into the territory where it becomes dangerous: judgment, strategy, creative direction, complex problem-solving. The work where your expertise is the differentiating input. For that category of work, the counterintuitive truth holds: the effort of pushing back, questioning, redirecting, catching plausible-but-wrong output isn't friction to eliminate. It's the multiplier in action. Remove the effort and you remove the value.

The evidence for this claim is strong enough to carry a chapter, with one caveat that comes up soon. It starts with a study we keep returning to, read this time through a different lens.

*

The Wharton-run experiment that Chapter 1 told as deskilling evidence has a second story inside it, and it's the one that matters most for Condition 2. The story is in the design. The tutor version refused to hand over solutions. It gave hints. It asked questions back. It required the student to do the cognitive work before receiving the tool's contribution. The tutor version was harder. Deliberately, structurally harder. And the harder path produced more than double the improvement during practice and no deskilling when the tool was removed, while the easy path left students below the peers who'd never had it.

Same tool. Same students. Same content. The only variable was how much cognitive work the collaboration demanded from the human. The easier path produced dependency. The harder path produced capability.

The learning science community has a name for this principle, and it predates the tools by thirty years. Robert Bjork formalized it in the early 1990s as "desirable difficulties": conditions that make learning harder during practice but improve long-term retention and transfer. Spacing, interleaving, retrieval practice: all of them slow you down in the moment and make you better over time. The Wharton scaffolded condition was a desirable difficulty applied to AI collaboration, and it produced exactly what the principle predicts. Nothing in this chapter is a discovery about difficulty. What's new is where the difficulty now has to come from.

Here's where this book extends the principle beyond the classroom. Desirable difficulties explains why the scaffolded condition worked for students learning new material. The claim here is that the same mechanism operates in professional collaboration, where the stakes aren't retention on an exam but the quality of the work you produce and the expertise you maintain. The effort of engaging with AI output, bringing your own judgment, catching errors, redirecting when the output is plausible but wrong, isn't just good pedagogy. It's the behavioral expression of Condition 2. It's what keeps x from collapsing.

Now the caveat, and it's the same one Chapter 1 made about deskilling. Most of the scaffolding evidence comes from educational contexts: students, learning tasks, controlled experiments. The extension to professional collaboration is H(x)AI's theoretical claim, supported by the direction of the evidence and not yet tested in a boardroom. The mechanism generalizes, or should; the data is thinner once you leave the classroom. Two studies come close to professional contexts, and both are worth the detail.

*

The seventy clinicians from the opening of Chapter 3 are the strongest professional case, and the effort lens shows why the structure worked. The critical rule, an independent assessment first, committed before seeing what the AI thought, created exactly the friction most clinicians, left to their own devices, would skip. Given the choice between forming your own assessment and then comparing, or just reading what the AI thinks and deciding whether you agree, most people take the easier path. The easier path is the one where the AI thinks first and the human nods along.

The protocol refused that path. It added time. It added cognitive load. It added the discomfort of committing to a diagnosis and discovering you were wrong. Accuracy improved anyway, because of the added work, not despite it. That's desirable difficulty applied to professional practice rather than a classroom, and it matters precisely because these weren't students learning algebra. These were practicing physicians making diagnostic decisions with real clinical implications. When the collaboration demands genuine cognitive engagement from the human, the output improves. When it doesn't, the human contribution quietly disappears.

A cross-country study by Gerlich tested the mechanism from the other direction: what happens when you don't structure the engagement? One hundred and fifty participants in Germany, Switzerland, and the UK used AI under two conditions. The unguided group used AI however they wanted: open-ended access, no framework, no required reflection. The structured group followed a prompting protocol designed to maintain reflective engagement. They had to articulate their own thinking at each stage, compare it to the AI's contribution, and explicitly decide what to keep and what to discard.

The results were not subtle. The unguided group fostered cognitive offloading without improving reasoning quality. They got faster at producing output, but the output didn't get better. The structured group reduced offloading and enhanced both critical reasoning and reflective engagement. Same tool, same task, same population. The only variable was whether the protocol required them to think before accepting.

The finding that deserves its own sentence: structured engagement also mitigated demographic disparities. Unstructured AI use amplified existing gaps between groups. Participants who started with fewer advantages drifted further behind when given unstructured access, because they had less existing expertise to notice when the AI was wrong. Structured engagement closed those gaps. The protocol created a floor of cognitive engagement that protected everyone, regardless of starting point.

The organizational implication is uncomfortable but clear: unstructured AI collaboration doesn't just produce worse average outcomes. It makes the playing field less level. The people who need the structure most are the ones least likely to create it for themselves.

*

So what does "harder" actually look like in practice?

Not artificial difficulty, and not making every interaction a struggle because struggle builds character. The difficulty that matters is the kind that maintains cognitive engagement. The effort that matters is specific: bringing your genuine expertise into the collaboration instead of leaving it in your head while you type a generic request.

The distinction is between process difficulty and cognitive engagement. Making the software interface clunky is process difficulty. Nobody benefits from that. Writing your own assessment before consulting the AI is cognitive engagement. Pushing back when the output contradicts your experience is cognitive engagement. Rejecting a recommendation because it doesn't account for something you know about the specific situation: cognitive engagement. All of these take time and energy. None of them is wasted.

Go back to the second architect from Chapter 4, the one who got the perforated-screen facade. The part of that scene that belongs to this chapter is what happened after the tool answered. She spent the next three hours pushing back on the structural assumptions and reworking the lobby circulation. She rejected output. She redirected. She refused a plausible-sounding suggestion because it didn't account for a constraint she knew and the tool didn't. Her process felt harder because it was harder. She wasn't struggling with the interface. She was doing what professionals do when they're engaged: bringing judgment, testing assumptions, refusing to accept output that didn't fit the specifics. That cognitive effort is the collaboration working. The moment it stops feeling like effort is the moment to ask whether you've stopped contributing.

That's Condition 2 in action. The collaboration demanded more of her. The "more" was the multiplier.

The claim has a scope, the same one Chapter 5 stated, and it travels with the claim. For judgment work, strategy, diagnosis, creative direction, any decision that turns on context: the human is the scarce input, the effort of bringing that input is what multiplies, and the mechanical layer around it can be handed to the tool without loss. For routine, well-specified execution, ease is the right feeling, the AI may well be the scarce input, and "harder is better" doesn't apply. For work that is mechanical all the way down, the honest word is displacement, and this book won't promise a hidden judgment layer where there isn't one. And for creative craft where the technique is the art, brushwork, sentence rhythm, a coder's style as a signature, the line between mechanical and essential is messy, and it's more honest to say so than to pretend the split is clean.

The question, then, isn't whether every AI interaction should be hard. The question is whether you can tell the difference between the interactions that should be effortless and the ones where effortlessness means you've stopped contributing.

*

Which brings us to the mechanism that makes this so difficult to see from the inside.

AI output is fluent, confident, and professionally formatted regardless of whether it's accurate. This is the fluency trap, and it operates with particular force in exactly the situations where Condition 2 matters most. When AI produces a competitive analysis that reads like a competitive analysis, your normal quality signals return a positive result. It's polished. It's coherent. The assertions sound confident. Every heuristic you've spent your career developing to evaluate the quality of professional work tells you this is fine.

But those heuristics were trained on human output, where polish correlates with effort and effort correlates with quality. AI breaks that correlation. Polish is the default, not the achievement. Confidence is the output style, not an indicator of accuracy. The signals you've relied on for decades to distinguish good work from bad work stop functioning as reliability indicators.

Chapter 2 told the story of the lawyers who filed fabricated citations, and Chapter 1 named what it was: a verification failure in one of the most verification-intensive professions on earth. Here the lawyers illustrate something more specific. The fluency trap is the mechanism that makes coasting invisible. When the output looks good regardless of whether you engaged with it, the only way to catch the quality gap is to bring your own expertise to the evaluation. That takes effort. The effort is the point.

A 2026 article in *California Management Review*'s Insight series named the organizational version of this dynamic with a term borrowed from economics: the Jevons Paradox. William Stanley Jevons observed in the 1860s that as coal engines became more efficient, total coal consumption went up, not down. Greater efficiency didn't reduce demand. It expanded use. Hamilton Mann's argument is that the same pattern applies to AI in organizations: as AI becomes more efficient at cognitive tasks, organizations expand its use, which erodes the human cognitive engagement that produces genuine value. AI substitutes for intermediate cognitive processes and desensitizes organizations to the effort those processes represent. The result is a confusion of efficiency with productivity. More output, produced faster, with less thinking. The metrics improve. The value degrades.

This is the Jevons Paradox applied to cognition. More efficient AI leads to expanded use, which leads to erosion of human faculties. Not because AI is harmful, but because the efficiency makes it easy to mistake volume for value.

*

The deskilling risk is downstream of the same mechanism.

The Wharton data showed it in an educational context: unrestricted, effortless AI access didn't just fail to build capability. It left students below the ones who never had the tool. The smaller retention study Chapter 1 mentioned points the same direction. And it's where the single-interaction habit Fernandes documented in Chapter 2 ends up: one question, one answer, done, and knowledge that doesn't stay.

Chapter 2 gave the professional version of the pattern a name: algorithmic loafing. The body stays present. The hands keep typing. The eyes keep scanning. The deliverables keep shipping. What drops out is the thinking. And the thinking, it turns out, is the part that matters.

Algorithmic loafing is invisible to every standard performance metric. You can't see it in task completion rates. You can't see it in output volume. You can't even see it by watching someone work, because the motor behavior looks identical to engagement. The only place it shows up is in the quality of the output, and only if you have enough domain expertise to tell the difference between competent and good. Between a competitive analysis that any consultant could produce and one that carries eleven years of judgment.

This connects directly to the deskilling pattern that Bainbridge identified in 1983, studying industrial automation: the more reliable the automated system, the more the human skills it needs as backup atrophy. She called it the "irony of automation." You automate precisely because humans are unreliable, and then the automation makes the humans more unreliable by removing the practice that kept their skills sharp. The irony compounds with AI because the degradation is invisible. A pilot who stops monitoring instruments eventually misses an alarm. A professional who stops engaging with AI output produces deliverables that look identical to engaged work until someone with domain expertise reads them carefully. The quality gap hides behind the polish.

When AI makes the work feel effortless, ask yourself the question that separates productive ease from dangerous ease: is the task routine, where efficiency is the point? Or does the task require my judgment, where effortlessness means I've stopped contributing?

Both feel the same from the inside. One of them is the multiplier working. The other is the multiplier collapsing.

*

The ease paradox deserves its own honest treatment, because the simple version of this argument gets it wrong.

The simple version says: if AI feels easy, you're doing it wrong. That's not the claim. Some experts find AI easy to use and get extraordinary results, because they've internalized the conditions so thoroughly that engagement is automatic. A seasoned trial lawyer who instantly sees the weakness in an AI-drafted argument isn't struggling. She's operating at a level where the judgment is reflexive. The effort happened over decades of practice. What she brings to the collaboration is effortless in the same way a concert pianist's technique is effortless: the difficulty has been absorbed into the skill.

The paradox is that genuine mastery and genuine disengagement produce the same subjective experience. Both feel easy. The difference is observable only in the output. The master's output carries the marks of expertise: specificity, judgment, the kind of insight that can only come from deep domain knowledge. The disengaged professional's output carries the marks of competence: professional, polished, and interchangeable with what anyone else would produce.

This is why Condition 2 is a practice and never a feeling. You can't check it by consulting your subjective experience. You check it by looking at the output and running Chapter 5's commodity test from the other side: is there anything here that the tool couldn't have generated from a generic request? Did my expertise, my knowledge of this specific situation, my judgment about what matters and what doesn't, actually make it into the final product? If the answer is yes, the ease is earned. If the answer is no, the ease is a signal.

The test is uncomfortable because it requires honesty about what you actually contributed. Not what you reviewed. Not what you approved. What you contributed. The consultant who reads an AI-generated competitive analysis, fixes two typos, and sends it to the client has reviewed. The one who wrote his own assessment first, challenged the AI's output against it, and revised both in light of the collision has contributed. The difference is visible in the output, even when both consultants feel equally productive.

*

Think about what this means for how organizations measure AI success.

If productive AI collaboration is harder, then measuring success by time saved or tasks completed faster is measuring the wrong thing. Speed might indicate efficiency on routine tasks. Good. Or it might indicate cognitive disengagement on judgment tasks. The 2025 developer telemetry from Chapter 1 showed exactly this: more tasks completed, more bugs shipped, no measurable company-level improvement. Faster and worse, but the dashboards only captured faster.

The Jevons Paradox compounds the measurement problem at scale. As AI efficiency improves, organizations naturally expand its use into higher-judgment work. Each expansion looks like productivity on a dashboard. Each expansion carries the risk that cognitive engagement drops without anyone noticing, because the fluency of the output masks the quality gap. The organization gets busier without getting better, and the metrics that would catch it (outcome quality, client-specific insight, strategic differentiation) are harder to measure than the metrics that hide it (volume, speed, adoption rate).

The uncomfortable implication for leaders: the teams reporting the smoothest AI integration might be the ones getting the least from it. Frictionless might mean the collaboration is working so well that expertise flows naturally into every interaction. Or frictionless might mean nobody's thinking anymore. You cannot distinguish between the two from the outside without looking at the output with expert eyes. The teams that report AI collaboration as "challenging" or "time-consuming" might be the ones doing it right, precisely because they're maintaining the cognitive engagement that produces genuine value.

This creates a measurement trap that most organizations haven't recognized. The metrics that are easy to capture (adoption rates, time savings, task throughput, user satisfaction) all point toward ease. They reward the teams that find AI frictionless. The metrics that would reveal quality (outcome differentiation, insight specificity, competitive advantage generated) require human judgment to assess and take months or years to manifest. By the time the quality gap shows up in business results, the habits are set and the expertise may have already degraded.

*

Return to the consultant from the top of this chapter.

He produced two competitive analyses. The first took forty-five minutes, felt productive, and could have come from anyone. The second took two hours, felt harder, and carried eleven years of pattern recognition, regulatory insight, and competitive judgment that no AI model possesses.

The difference between those two drafts is Condition 2. The first draft let the tool do the work. The second demanded that he do more work than he would have done alone: he wrote his own assessment, then challenged it against the AI's, then pushed back, then revised. The collaboration didn't replace his effort. It multiplied it. And the multiplication only worked because he brought something worth multiplying.

That's the counterintuitive truth at the heart of this condition. The people who treat AI as a labor-saving device for judgment work are saving exactly the labor that produces the value. The people who find AI collaboration genuinely demanding, who push back, who bring their own thinking before accepting the tool's, who spend more time on the AI-assisted version than they would have on the unassisted one, are the people who get results nobody else can replicate.

The collaboration demands more of you, not less. That's not a bug. It's the mechanism.

The next question is what happens when the effort you bring runs headlong into a deeper challenge: not just doing more work, but confronting what the work reveals about who you are and what your expertise actually is. That's Condition 3, and it's the one most people would rather not think about.

Notes

1. Bastani, H., Bastani, O., Sungu, A., Ge, H., Kabakcı, Ö., & Mariman, R. (2025). "Generative AI without guardrails can harm learning: Evidence from high school mathematics." *Proceedings of the National Academy of Sciences*, 122(26), e2422633122. DOI: 10.1073/pnas.2422633122. See Chapter 1, Note 12 for the figures.
2. Bjork, R.A. (1994). "Memory and metamemory considerations in the training of human beings." In J. Metcalfe & A.P. Shimamura (Eds.), *Metacognition: Knowing About Knowing* (pp. 185-205). MIT Press.
3. Everett, S.S., et al. (2026). "From tool to teammate in a randomized controlled trial of clinician-AI collaborative workflows for diagnosis." *npj Digital Medicine*, 9, 409. DOI: 10.1038/s41746-026-02545-1. Full author list in Chapter 3, Note 1.
4. Gerlich, M. (2025). "From offloading to engagement: An experimental study on structured prompting and critical reasoning with generative AI." *Data*, 10(11), 172. DOI: 10.3390/data10110172. Cross-country experiment, n=150 (Germany, Switzerland, UK).
5. Mann, H. (2026). "AI Productivity Blind Spot." *California Management Review Insight*, January 26, 2026.
6. Bainbridge, L. (1983). "Ironies of automation." *Automatica*, 19(6), 775-779.
7. Faros AI (2025). "The AI Productivity Paradox." Published July 23, 2025. See Chapter 1, Note 4.

CHAPTER 7

My Professional Identity Is Clarified, Not Threatened

Fifteen years of financial models. That's what Maria built her reputation on. The most thorough models in the department: layered assumptions, sensitivity analyses that anticipated questions the board hadn't thought to ask, revenue projections wired to contract milestones that only someone who'd read every deal memo could have specified. When people in the organization needed to understand what the numbers meant, they came to Maria. And what Maria understood about herself, the story she carried into every meeting and every performance review, was simple: I am the person who builds these models.

Then a junior analyst showed her what the new AI tools could produce in eleven minutes.

The architecture was clean. The sensitivity tables were formatted correctly. The output looked, at first glance, like something that would have taken Maria most of a day. Her first reaction wasn't curiosity. It wasn't excitement about the time she'd save. It was a feeling she couldn't name immediately, something between vertigo and anger: if anyone with a subscription can build what I build, then what am I?

That question is the subject of this chapter. Maria is a construction; no single analyst lived exactly this arc, but every profession has its version of her, and the mechanism her story walks through is the documented one. And the answer turns out to be more interesting, and more liberating, than most people expect.

Here's what I keep landing on when I look at the identity research: the threat is real, the fear is rational, and the crisis is productive. Most professionals experiencing it don't know that last part yet.

*

The feeling Maria experienced has a name in the research literature, and it operates independently of everything else organizations try to address when they roll out AI.

Mirbabaie and colleagues studied what happens psychologically when professionals encounter AI that can perform components of their work. They identified three central predictors of AI-related identity threat: changes to the nature of work itself, perceived loss of status or position, and what the researchers called "AI identity," how individuals see themselves in relation to AI systems. The critical finding wasn't that identity threat exists. Everyone who's watched a senior professional dismiss AI tools with "I didn't get where I am by trusting machines" already knows that. The critical finding was that identity threat is *independent*. It operates on its own channel. It's not reducible to resistance to change, lack of AI knowledge, or fear of job loss. You can address all three of those and still have the identity problem, untouched, still in the way.

That word matters: independent. It means you can run a perfect change management process, provide excellent training, communicate the benefits clearly, build psychological safety around experimentation, and the senior consultant who has spent twenty years defining herself through the quality of her strategic analysis will still avoid using AI for client-facing work. She understands the tool. The rollout was competent. The avoidance is about something else: using the tool for the work that defines her professional identity feels like an admission that two decades of expertise aren't sufficient.

This isn't a character flaw. It's a protection mechanism. And it's measurable.

Hermann, Puntoni, and Morewedge published a framework in *Trends in Cognitive Sciences* that maps the mechanism precisely. Generative AI threatens three basic psychological needs: competence (can I still do valuable work?), autonomy (am I still in control of how I work?), and relatedness (do I still belong in my professional community?). When those needs are threatened, three of the coping strategies that emerge, dissociation, escapism, symbolic self-completion, are the clinical names for what looks like "resistance" in a boardroom. The senior partner who uses AI only for document review but never for case strategy isn't resisting technology. He's protecting his sense of professional competence in the only domain where it still feels fully his.

*

Reif, Larrick, and Soll tested the social dimension of this dynamic across four preregistered experiments with 4,439 participants. Their finding: using AI resulted in a 9 percent lower competence rating from peers. That's the baseline penalty for being seen to collaborate with AI tools on professional tasks. But the penalty isn't distributed evenly. For women in engineering roles, the competence penalty was 13 percent. And when male non-adopters evaluated female engineers who used AI, the penalty hit 26 percent.

Sit with that number. A quarter of your perceived professional competence, erased, because you used a tool that the organization presumably wants you to use.

The competence penalty makes identity threat structural, not just personal. Even if Maria resolves her own identity question, if she figures out what her expertise actually is and brings it confidently into AI collaboration, the social environment may still punish her for it. The fear is calibrated to a real cost, measured across four preregistered experiments and published. When organizations wonder why their AI adoption stalls among senior professionals, especially women, part of the answer lives in social dynamics that training rarely reaches.

A research team studying faculty attitudes toward AI found that over a third opted out entirely. When the researchers analyzed the reasons, one category stood apart from the rest: "identity in tension." Not lack of training. Not philosophical objection. A specific, articulable feeling that the tool's capabilities called into question the capabilities they'd built careers around. Faculty members in fields where AI could generate passable first drafts of lectures, grade student work, or produce research summaries experienced the tool as a challenge to who they were, not just what they did.

Identity threat doesn't announce itself as identity threat. It shows up wearing other clothes: "The tool isn't there yet for strategic work." "I prefer my own process." "AI doesn't understand nuance." These aren't lies. The people saying them believe them. But underneath the rational-sounding explanation is a simpler, harder truth: if this tool can do what I do, then the story I tell about why I'm valuable needs to change. And nobody changes that story voluntarily without a reason.

*

So what does AI actually take away? The question matters because the answer isn't "everything." It's something much more specific, and much less catastrophic, than most professionals fear.

The conventional narrative offers two framings, and both are wrong. The optimistic version: "AI won't replace you, it will augment you." This is reassurance. It stops being comforting the first time you watch AI produce something that looks indistinguishable from your best work. The pessimistic version: "AI will replace most knowledge work within a decade." This is catastrophizing. It treats all professional contribution as a single undifferentiated block that either gets automated or doesn't.

Neither framing helps Maria at 2 a.m. when she's staring at a model AI built in eleven minutes that took her a day.

What helps is a more precise question: what, specifically, does AI commoditize, and what, specifically, remains?

Go back to Maria. After the initial shock, she did what many professionals do in the surrender phase: she stopped building models and let AI handle it. She became an editor of AI output rather than a creator of her own. The work was faster. It was also worse. The models lacked something she hadn't consciously noticed she was contributing: dozens of embedded judgment calls, built from years of working with specific clients in specific industries, that never appeared in any formula or instruction set.

The shift came three months later. A junior analyst brought Maria an AI-generated model for a client whose contracts had unusual milestone-based revenue triggers. The model looked clean. The formatting was professional. And the revenue recognition timing was subtly wrong in a way that would have produced a materially misleading projection.

Maria caught it in seconds, and she wasn't auditing for errors. She *knew* this client. She knew the milestone triggers were tied to regulatory approvals that historically came in waves, not on the linear schedule the model assumed. That knowledge was judgment, built over a decade of watching how this industry actually worked, as opposed to how it was supposed to work on paper.

The moment she caught the error was the moment her identity clarified. Not in words. Nobody sits in a conference room and thinks "my professional identity has shifted from mechanical execution to contextual judgment." It was quieter than that. She looked at the model, saw the error, and realized that what she'd been mourning, the speed, the architecture, the mechanical precision of building the model from scratch, wasn't her expertise at all. It was the scaffolding around her expertise. The spreadsheets were the vehicle. The understanding was the destination.

What Maria actually brought, what no tool could replicate, was the contextual understanding of what the numbers meant for this specific business in this specific market with these specific contract structures. The mechanical output got commoditized. The essential contribution became visible.

I love that moment in the story. Not because it's dramatic. Because it's so quiet. The loudest identity shifts usually are.

*

The distinction between mechanical and essential is where this argument either builds trust or loses it. Because the line isn't always clean, and pretending otherwise is the fastest way to sound like someone selling motivational reassurance rather than telling the truth.

So before the argument goes further, the scope has to be stated, the same scope Chapters 5 and 6 carried, because it travels with the claim. For judgment work, strategy, diagnosis, creative direction, any decision that turns on context: the human is the scarce input, the effort of bringing that input is what multiplies, and the mechanical layer around it can be handed to the tool without loss. For routine, well-specified execution, ease is the right feeling, the AI may well be the scarce input, and "harder is better" doesn't apply. For work that is mechanical all the way down, the honest word is displacement, and this book won't promise a hidden judgment layer where there isn't one. And for creative craft where the technique is the art, brushwork, sentence rhythm, a coder's style as a signature, the line between mechanical and essential is messy, and it's more honest to say so than to pretend the split is clean.

That third category deserves one more sentence here, because this is the identity chapter and identity is where false comfort does the most damage. For the data-entry specialist whose entire role is accurate transcription from one format to another, the production-line worker whose value was precision and speed on a repeatable task, the filing clerk, the basic accounts-payable processor: the mechanical *was* the job, and the labor-market consequence is real even when the displacement arrives gradually rather than all at once. Dressing that up as "an opportunity for growth" would be dishonest, and this chapter won't.

The chapter is addressed instead to the much larger category of professionals whose work *does* have a judgment layer, and who haven't recognized its value because the mechanical components were always more visible, more measurable, and more rewarded. The financial analyst who thinks she builds spreadsheets when she actually understands businesses. The lawyer who thinks he drafts contracts when he actually manages risk. The marketer who thinks she writes copy when she actually understands audiences. The architect who thinks she produces drawings when she actually solves spatial problems under constraint. For that category the mechanical-vs-essential distinction makes the identity story move from threat to clarification. The argument below is bounded to that category, not extended past it. And for the fourth category, the writer whose sentences are the work, the painter whose hand is the point, the developer whose style is a signature: the argument below applies in part, and this book would rather admit that than pretend the line runs cleanly through a craft where the technique and the judgment were never separate.

With that scope in place, here is the honest version: AI commoditizes the reproducible components of expertise. The parts of your work that follow patterns, that can be specified as rules, that produce similar outputs regardless of who performs them. Spreadsheet construction. First-draft generation. Standard research synthesis. Data formatting. Template application. Code that follows established patterns. These are mechanical not because they're easy, but because they're reproducible: given the same inputs and the same rules, anyone competent arrives at the same output.

What remains after the mechanical is commoditized is what was never reproducible in the first place: the judgment calls that depend on context nobody else has, the taste that distinguishes work that resonates from work that merely functions, the ethical reasoning that weighs competing obligations, the creative vision that connects disparate elements into something that didn't exist before, the contextual understanding that comes from years inside a specific domain watching how things actually work versus how models predict they should work.

These become *more* valuable when the mechanical is commoditized. Not less. Because when everyone has access to the same mechanical output (and they do, because the tool is the same tool), the only thing that differentiates one professional's work from another's is the non-mechanical contribution. The judgment layer becomes the entire margin.

Brynjolfsson, Li, and Raymond studied over five thousand customer support agents working alongside AI and found that the tool compressed the skill distribution: novice agents improved dramatically, experienced agents barely changed. The standard interpretation frames this as "AI helps beginners more." Chapter 4 offered one other reading. Read it through an identity lens and a third story is available, and it's a reading, not something the study measured. What happened to those experienced agents? Their procedural knowledge, the mechanical component that used to take years to accumulate, got commoditized overnight. A new agent with AI could match their speed and accuracy on routine interactions. The experienced agents' value didn't disappear. It relocated. Their worth shifted to what the AI couldn't provide: contextual judgment about when a routine situation was actually non-routine, relationship management with escalated customers, complex problem-solving where the right answer wasn't in any knowledge base. The mechanical got commoditized. The essential became the differentiator.

That's clarification, not diminishment. But only if you can see it happening. And most professionals, in the moment, can't.

Here's why. Organizations have rewarded the mechanical components of expertise for decades, speed, volume, technical execution, because those components were visible, measurable, and scarce before AI. The financial analyst who could build a complex model faster than her peers was genuinely more valuable. The lawyer who could draft a contract from memory was genuinely more efficient. The marketer who could produce clean copy on deadline was genuinely productive. The mechanical skills deserved the recognition they got. The problem is that identity followed the rewards. Professionals built their self-concept around the thing that got noticed, which was the mechanical output, not the judgment that guided it. Nobody told them they were building on the wrong layer. It wasn't the wrong layer. Not then.

Now it is. And the disorientation isn't stupidity or stubbornness. It's the rational response to having the foundation of your professional identity reclassified overnight from "scarce" to "commodity." For the professionals this chapter addresses, the identity threat is real, but the identity crisis is productive. It's pointing at something worth discovering. The discomfort is a sign that something important is trying to surface.

*

There's a second pathway through this transition that the "reveal" metaphor doesn't capture.

Picture a marketing coordinator, twenty-eight years old, three years into his career. He hasn't accumulated a decade of contextual judgment to reveal. He can't strip away the mechanical and find deep expertise underneath because he's still building that expertise. The reveal metaphor doesn't fit his experience. Something else does.

AI handles the mechanical tasks he used to spend 60 percent of his time on: formatting presentations, assembling basic research summaries, scheduling content calendars, pulling data into standard reports. That time is now free. And what fills it isn't a revelation of hidden capability. It's an acceleration of construction. He spends more hours on strategy conversations. He sits in more client meetings. He takes on higher-judgment work earlier in his career than any previous cohort of marketers could have.

He's not uncovering a hidden identity. He's building a new one, with AI as the catalyst that freed the time he needed to build it.

Herminia Ibarra's research on professional identity describes this pathway with precision: identity isn't a stable core waiting to be uncovered. It's constructed iteratively through experimentation. People try possible selves, test them against the reactions of others and their own sense of fit, and gradually build a professional identity that feels authentic. For early-career professionals in the AI transition, Condition 3 looks less like revelation and more like accelerated construction. Both pathways arrive at the same destination: an identity grounded in what you uniquely contribute, clarified rather than threatened by AI's presence.

The experienced analyst who recognizes her judgment when the mechanical is stripped away is traveling the reveal path. The junior coordinator who builds his expertise faster because the mechanical no longer consumes his time is traveling the construct path. Both are real. Both lead to the same place. Clarified.

*

The distinction between these pathways matters because the emotional experience is different, and the support each requires is different too.

The reveal path often involves grief. Real grief, not the motivational-poster kind. Maria mourned the identity she'd built around spreadsheet architecture before she could see what was underneath. She'd spent fifteen years perfecting something that was, in retrospect, the container rather than the contents. That's a loss worth mourning, even when what's revealed underneath is more valuable. Anyone who's been through therapy recognizes the structure: letting go of a protective story about yourself is painful even when the story was limiting you.

The construct path involves excitement mixed with uncertainty. The coordinator knows he's building something, but he can't yet see its final shape. He doesn't have the settled confidence of the experienced professional who's discovered her core. He's experimenting, trying on possible professional selves, Ibarra's language, and figuring out which ones fit. The uncertainty is productive, but it's still uncertainty.

What both pathways share is a common mechanism: the resolution of threat into clarity. Shonhe and Min studied this transition and found two factors that consistently reduce professional identity threat from AI. The first is explainability: when professionals understand what AI is doing and why, the tool becomes less threatening because it becomes less opaque. The second, and more interesting, is what the researchers called "AI identity," how individuals conceptualize their relationship to AI systems. When professionals develop a clear sense of who they are *in relation to* AI, a stable understanding of what they contribute and what the tool contributes, the threat diminishes and engagement becomes adaptive rather than defensive.

That's Condition 3 in research language. When the relationship clarifies, when the professional knows their role in the collaboration, the threat resolves. The threat was real and remains real; what changes is the recognition that it was pointing at something: a need to clarify what "professional expertise" actually means in a world where the mechanical components are no longer scarce.

*

The clarification doesn't happen automatically. That's worth stating directly, because the narrative arc from "threat" to "clarity" can sound like an inevitable progression. It isn't.

Plenty of professionals stay stuck in threat indefinitely, protecting an identity built on the wrong layer while their work slowly becomes indistinguishable from what any competent person with a subscription could produce. They're the Defenders from Chapter 9's typology: senior professionals whose expertise is real, whose protectiveness is understandable, and whose cost is invisible to them. They'll never discover what AI could have added to their judgment because they never let it close enough to find out. The defend-and-avoid pattern is stable. It doesn't collapse on its own. It just quietly produces mediocrity where excellence used to live.

What moves professionals from threat to clarity is some version of what happened to Maria: an encounter that makes the judgment layer visible. For Maria, it was catching an error that AI couldn't catch. For others, it's a client who says "anyone could have produced this first draft, but only you knew which assumptions to challenge." For still others, it's the negative version: noticing that their AI-assisted work has become generic, that the distinctive quality they used to produce has silently disappeared, and asking why.

The encounter can't be manufactured through training. You can't lecture someone into seeing their own judgment layer. But you can create conditions where the encounter is more likely: structured collaboration where the human is explicitly positioned as the contributor of judgment, reflection practices that make the mechanical/essential distinction visible, environments where the social penalty for AI use doesn't make the whole question too dangerous to explore.

Remember the competence penalty from earlier in this chapter. Those numbers describe an environment where the identity question is too dangerous to even approach. If the social cost of using AI can be a quarter of your perceived professional competence, you're not going to experiment with what your expertise looks like on the other side of AI collaboration. You're going to protect what you have. Condition 3 can't operate in an environment that punishes the behavior it requires. Which is why psychological safety, Chapter 10's territory, isn't a nice-to-have for identity clarification. It's infrastructure.

That's what Condition 3 provides. Not the answer to "what is my expertise?" That answer is different for everyone, and nobody can hand it to you. What Condition 3 provides is the psychological permission to ask the question without feeling like the answer will be "nothing." Reassurance ("AI won't replace you") expires the first time the tool produces something uncomfortably good. Training ("learn new skills") doesn't touch identity. The reframe is something else: AI reveals what your expertise always actually was. Or, for those still building: AI creates the conditions to build the expertise that matters most.

Same data, different meaning. And the different meaning changes everything about how someone shows up in the collaboration.

*

The connection back to x runs through everything in this chapter. Identity threat suppresses the mental model multiplier. When a professional feels threatened by AI, two things happen, and both collapse the collaboration.

The threatened professional who surrenders stops contributing. If the tool can do what I do, why bring my judgment at all? This is a direct hit to Condition 1: the belief that you are the scarce input. When identity threat is active, Condition 1 becomes psychologically unavailable. You can't believe your contribution is essential when you're not sure your contribution has value.

The threatened professional who fights refuses to let AI contribute. If letting the tool into my domain means admitting my expertise isn't sufficient, I'll keep the tool out. This is a hit to Conditions 2 and 4: the willingness to engage in difficult collaboration and the willingness to calibrate. When identity is at stake, honest engagement feels like self-destruction.

Both paths produce the same outcome: x drops. Not because the professional lacks capability, but because the capability stays locked behind an identity they're too threatened to reexamine.

Condition 3 removes the suppression. When the professional sees AI as clarifying rather than threatening, the psychological barriers dissolve. Contributing expertise doesn't feel like admitting inadequacy (C1 becomes available). Engaging deeply with AI output doesn't feel like surrendering professional territory (C2 becomes available). And calibrating honestly, admitting where AI adds value and where it doesn't, stops feeling like a concession and starts feeling like professional practice (C4 becomes available).

Identity is the condition that unlocks the other three. The psychological heart of the multiplier.

Which is why AI training, prompt engineering instruction, and change management process won't close the gap Chapter 1 documented on their own, not until the identity question gets addressed. You can teach someone everything about AI and they'll still hold back if using the tool threatens who they believe they are. You can build the best collaboration framework in the world and they'll still coast through it on autopilot if engaging deeply means confronting a professional identity they're not ready to reexamine. The identity question is load-bearing. However the other conditions develop, they hold or fail on how it's resolved.

*

Think about the financial analyst again, but with the new lens this chapter provides.

Before clarification, Maria's identity was "the person who builds the best financial models in the department." AI threatened that identity directly, and the threat produced predictable responses: first resistance, then surrender, then generic work that happened to be fast. Her x was near zero, not because she lacked expertise but because the expertise was locked behind an identity crisis she hadn't resolved.

After clarification, Maria's identity is "the person who understands what the numbers mean for this business." AI handles the mechanical construction. Maria provides the judgment that makes the output meaningful rather than merely correct. Her contribution is more visible than before, not less, because the mechanical scaffolding no longer obscures it. Her x moved because her identity moved.

The spreadsheet was always just the vehicle. The expertise was always the destination. AI stripped away the vehicle and revealed the destination. Or, for the coordinator still building his career: AI cleared the road so he could reach the destination faster.

Both stories end the same way: professional identity clarified.

AI changes what your expertise looks like; that part is settled. The question is whether you can see what was always underneath the mechanical, or build what becomes possible when the mechanical is handled. That is an identity question, and identity questions don't resolve through training, better prompts, or change management. They resolve through the kind of honest self-examination that most organizations have never asked of their professionals, and that most professionals have never asked of themselves. The next chapter is about how you keep that examination honest once the tools start moving under you.

Notes

1. Mirbabaie, M., Brünker, F., Möllmann Frick, N.R.J., & Stieglitz, S. (2022). "The rise of artificial intelligence – understanding the AI identity threat at the workplace." *Electronic Markets*, 32(1), 73-99. DOI: 10.1007/s12525-021-00496-x.
2. Reif, J.A., Larrick, R.P., & Soll, J.B. (2025). "Evidence of a social evaluation penalty for using AI." *Proceedings of the National Academy of Sciences*, 122(19), e2426766122. DOI: 10.1073/pnas.2426766122. Four preregistered experiments, 4,439 participants; 9% competence penalty overall; 13% for women in engineering; 26% when male non-adopters rated female engineers.

3. Hermann, E., Puntoni, S., & Morewedge, C.K. (2025). "GenAI and the psychology of work." *Trends in Cognitive Sciences*, 29(9). DOI: 10.1016/j.tics.2025.04.009.

4. Shata, A. (2025). "'Opting out of AI': Exploring perceptions, reasons, and concerns behind faculty resistance to generative AI." *Frontiers in Communication*, 10, 1614804. DOI: 10.3389/fcomm.2025.1614804.

5. Brynjolfsson, E., Li, D., & Raymond, L. (2023). "Generative AI at Work." NBER Working Paper No. 31161; published in *The Quarterly Journal of Economics* (2025). 5,179 agents; the "relocation" reading in the text is the book's interpretation, not a result reported by the study.

6. Ibarra, H. (2003). *Working Identity: Unconventional Strategies for Reinventing Your Career*. Harvard Business School Press.

7. Shonhe, L. & Min, J. (2025). "Mitigating AI-induced professional identity threat and fostering adoption in the workplace." *AI & Society*, 40, 4079-4092. DOI: 10.1007/s00146-024-02170-0.

CHAPTER 8

Calibration Is a Continuous Practice

Forty-four percent of the people who quit said the same thing: they didn't trust the answers.

Not because Microsoft Copilot was too expensive. Not because they didn't understand how to use it. Not because their organizations failed to train them. The people who tried one of the most heavily resourced AI products in history and walked away, in a 2025 survey of lapsed users, couldn't tell when the tool was reliable and when it wasn't. So they stopped using it entirely.

That number sits in a market report like any other churn metric, but read it as a psychological diagnosis and the story changes. These weren't technophobes. They'd adopted the tool voluntarily, used it long enough to form an opinion, and then made a rational calculation: the cost of trusting unreliable output exceeded the benefit of occasional good output, and they had no way to separate the two. No method, no practice, no framework for knowing when to trust and when to doubt. Without calibration, trust defaults to a binary: all or nothing. Total acceptance or total rejection. The surrenderers and the fighters from the Introduction, showing up one more time in enterprise telemetry.

The previous three chapters explored conditions that change how you relate to AI: seeing yourself as the essential contributor, embracing the effort productive collaboration requires, allowing your professional identity to be clarified rather than threatened. Each condition shifts something structural about the mental model. But none of them answers a question the reader has probably been carrying since Chapter 5: how do you know when you're right?

You can believe you're the scarce input and still be wrong about what you're contributing. You can invest genuine effort and still push back on the wrong things. You can feel clarified about your identity and still hold outdated assumptions about where AI excels and where it fails. The first three conditions create the psychological readiness for productive collaboration. The fourth condition keeps it honest.

Calibration. Not confidence. Not distrust. The ongoing practice of checking whether your model of AI's capabilities matches reality, and adjusting when it doesn't. It's the AI-facing half of the coupling: the first three conditions govern what you bring, and this one governs what you're able to draw out.

*

The distinction between confidence and calibration is worth drawing precisely, because people conflate them constantly and the conflation is where most failures hide.

Confidence is a feeling: I believe this AI output is correct. Or: I believe this AI tool is generally reliable for this kind of work. Confidence has a direction (positive or negative) and an intensity (strong or weak), and it tells you almost nothing about whether the thing you believe is true.

Calibration is a correspondence: the degree to which your confidence tracks actual accuracy. A well-calibrated person who says "I'm 80 percent sure this output is right" is right approximately 80 percent of the time. A poorly calibrated person who says the same thing might be right 40 percent of the time, or 95 percent of the time. Both feel equally confident. Only one knows what that confidence is worth.

Lee and colleagues, writing in *PNAS Nexus*, formalized this distinction in the context of AI trust. They studied what they called metacognitive sensitivity: the correspondence between a person's confidence judgments and their actual accuracy when evaluating AI outputs. The finding that matters: when AI provides high confidence ratings, humans correspondingly increase their trust, even when the AI is wrong. The confidence signal from the machine overrides the human's independent judgment. Their argument is that a confidence number alone can't fix this; what the human needs is a read on how well the tool's confidence tracks its accuracy, and a read on how well their own does.

That's one way to read the Copilot distrust data, and it's the reading this chapter takes. The 44 percent who quit weren't uniquely suspicious people. Plausibly, they were people whose sense that something was off was accurate, but who lacked the tools to do anything about it except leave. They could feel the unreliability. They couldn't localize it, predict it, or manage around it. Without a calibration practice, the only rational response to noticed-but-unmanageable unreliability is withdrawal.

The people who stayed and thrived aren't more trusting. They're better calibrated. They've built a working model of where Copilot is reliable and where it isn't, for their specific tasks, in their specific domain. They check. They update. They treat their model of AI's capabilities as a hypothesis under continuous revision, not as a settled belief.

*

This is where calibration parts company with most of what the AI training industry currently offers.

The dominant intervention for AI overreliance is education: teach people about AI's limitations, and they'll be more careful. Show them examples of hallucinations. Explain how models work. The logic is straightforward: if people know AI can be wrong, they'll check more carefully.

The studies that have tried a different approach point the other way. In 2021, before ChatGPT, Zana Buçinca and colleagues at Harvard tested what they called cognitive forcing functions against the standard fix of the day, explaining the AI's reasoning. Three forcing designs, two explanation designs, one no-AI baseline. The forcing designs cut overreliance substantially; the explanations barely moved it. Two other results from that study belong in this book. Participants gave the lowest ratings to the designs that helped them most: the intervention that reduced overreliance the most was the one people liked least, which is Chapter 6's argument in a lab. And the benefit skewed toward people who already liked to think hard, which is Chapter 10's problem in miniature.

A cognitive forcing function is a structural intervention that changes the sequence of cognition rather than its content. Instead of telling people "remember to check AI's work" (knowledge), a forcing function makes it impossible to proceed without first engaging your own judgment (structure). The difference is between a sign that says "look both ways" and a speed bump that forces you to slow down. One provides information. The other changes behavior by changing the environment.

The clinician workflow from Chapter 3 makes this concrete, because it was a forcing function and nothing else: independent assessment first, recorded and committed, before the AI's recommendation became visible.

The intervention wasn't training. Nobody learned more about AI. Nobody received a lecture on automation bias. The only change was structural: you had to think first, before the AI's confident output could anchor you. And it worked. Diagnostic accuracy improved over clinicians working with conventional resources. The clinicians' attitudes toward AI never changed; the cognitive sequence prevented the anchoring that makes AI output so difficult to evaluate independently.

This is the behavioral expression of calibration. Not "remember to be careful" but "structure your process so that your own judgment exists independently before AI's judgment can influence it." The distinction maps directly onto what Chapter 2 established about surface versus depth: knowledge interventions tell you what to do. Structural interventions make you do it. The clinician study addressed Condition 2 (maintained cognitive engagement) and Condition 4 (required independent assessment) simultaneously. Two conditions at once.

No study has lined these interventions up head to head; the comparison runs across different rooms, different tasks, different measures. But the direction is hard to miss: the knowledge-only interventions keep failing, and the intervention that reached two conditions at once is the one that moved accuracy. That's not proof of the system claim this chapter will make. It's consistent with it, and that's as far as it goes.

*

The forcing function research illuminates something uncomfortable about how most people currently relate to AI: the default cognitive sequence is backwards.

Here's what typically happens: you open the tool, type a request, receive an output, and then try to evaluate it. But the output is already there. It's polished, confident, and specific. Your brain processes it as a first draft that needs editing, not as a hypothesis that needs testing. The anchoring has already occurred by the time you begin your "evaluation." You're not checking AI's work from a position of independent judgment. You're trying to find problems with a conclusion you've already half-accepted.

A calibration practice reverses this. It doesn't require you to distrust AI or to slow everything down. It requires you to know, before you open the tool, what you think. To have a hypothesis, a standard, a sense of what good looks like for this specific task. Then AI's output becomes something you compare against your own thinking rather than something you react to in a vacuum.

Picture a product manager who works with AI daily on competitive analysis, market sizing, strategic recommendations. She builds a ten-minute weekly practice, the weekly calibration loop: pick one AI-assisted decision from the past week, one that actually played out. Check the outcome against what the AI recommended and against what she contributed. Was her trust well-placed? Did she catch what needed catching? Did AI perform better or worse than she expected in this specific domain?

Over weeks, her model of AI's strengths and weaknesses becomes empirically grounded rather than impression-based. She discovers patterns: AI's market sizing overestimates by roughly 15 percent for her segment, consistently. AI's competitive analysis is strong on public data but misses organizational dynamics that aren't in any dataset. AI's strategic recommendations are good starting points but rarely account for the specific relationship dynamics between her company and its partners.

None of this was available to her from training. No certification program could have told her where AI is reliable for *her* work. The calibration is specific to her domain, her tools, her context. It's empirical, not theoretical. And it compounds: each week's check refines her model, making next week's collaboration more precise.

This is what calibration looks like when it's a practice rather than a feeling: no anxiety about AI's reliability, no paranoia about being fooled, just a regular, deliberate feedback loop that keeps her mental model of AI's capabilities grounded in observed performance rather than hope or fear.

*

The difference between calibration and anxiety deserves its own beat, because people conflate them and the conflation is paralyzing. Anxiety asks: "What if AI is wrong? What if I'm being fooled? What if this output looks right but isn't?" It's reactive, generalized, and exhausting. It makes every interaction feel like a test you might fail. People who approach AI with anxiety either check everything obsessively (unsustainable, burns out within weeks) or stop checking entirely because the cognitive load is too high (surrender by another path).

Calibration says: "Based on my last ten interactions in this domain, AI gets market sizing wrong about 15 percent of the time and gets competitive positioning right about 80 percent of the time. For this specific task, I need to verify the sizing and can probably trust the positioning." Calibration is proactive, specific, and energy-neutral. It's not more work. It's better-targeted work. You check the things that need checking and trust the things you've earned the right to trust.

The anxious user checks everything or nothing. The calibrated user checks the right things. Same total effort. Vastly different outcomes. And calibration has a property that anxiety lacks: it improves over time. Each calibration check adds data. The model gets more precise. The effort decreases as confidence becomes warranted rather than assumed. An anxious relationship with AI gets worse with use. A calibrated one gets better.

*

AI capabilities change. This is obvious but its implications for calibration are not.

A data scientist evaluates AI coding tools when they first launch. She tests them on complex statistical modeling: the kind of work where subtle errors in implementation produce results that look plausible but are mathematically wrong. She finds the tools unreliable for this purpose. Fair assessment. She stops using them for statistical work and moves on.

Eighteen months later, the tools have improved dramatically for exactly this use case. Model architectures changed. Training data expanded. The specific weakness she identified has been addressed across two major version updates. She doesn't know because she never rechecked. Her calibration froze in 2024 while the tools moved on.

She's not resistant. She's not a fighter. She made a reasonable, evidence-based judgment that was accurate at the time. The problem is that calibration has a shelf life. AI capabilities shift quarterly. Your model of those capabilities drifts out of alignment invisibly, because nothing in your environment signals the change. The tool doesn't send a notification: "That thing you decided I couldn't do? I can do it now." The drift is silent.

This is the Drifter from Chapter 9's failure modes, and it's worth naming here because it's the failure mode that calibration specifically prevents. The Drifter isn't low on any of the first three conditions. She might believe she's the scarce input, invest genuine effort, and feel clear about her professional identity. What she lacks is the ongoing check: Has AI gotten better at this since I last tested? Has it gotten worse? Am I bringing my expertise to bear on the right tasks, or am I protecting territory I no longer need to protect?

Without active recalibration, your mental model degrades toward whichever assessment you made first. Initial impressions fossilize. And because AI changes faster than any previous tool category, the degradation happens faster too. A calibration practice isn't optional maintenance. It's the mechanism that keeps the other three conditions grounded in reality rather than memory.

*

There's a reason the drift is so hard to notice, and a field experiment made it visible in a way no argument could.

In 2023, a team from Harvard, Wharton, and MIT ran an experiment with 758 consultants at Boston Consulting Group, roughly seven percent of the firm's consulting staff at the time. The consultants were given eighteen realistic tasks, the kind of work they did every day: generating product ideas, writing marketing copy, analyzing a business problem from interview notes and spreadsheets. Some worked with GPT-4. Some didn't. Nothing about the AI was customized; it was the model anyone could have used in the fall of 2023.

For most of the tasks, the results were what the vendors promise. Consultants with AI finished 12.2 percent more tasks, 25.1 percent faster, and independent graders rated their output about 40 percent higher in quality. The gains were largest for the consultants who had scored lowest on a baseline assessment, which is Brynjolfsson's compression finding again, in a different industry.

Then there was the one task the researchers had built to sit just past what the model could do: a business-analysis problem where the right answer required weighing qualitative interview notes against numbers in a way GPT-4 got subtly wrong. Consultants who used AI on that task were 19 percentage points less likely to reach the correct answer than consultants working alone. Same tool. Same people. Same afternoon. On seventeen tasks it made them better; on the eighteenth it made them worse, and it did so fluently.

The researchers named the shape of that finding the jagged technological frontier. AI's capability is a coastline, not a line that advances evenly across all work. Some tasks that look hard sit well inside what the model can do; some tasks that look easy sit just outside it. From where the consultant stands, the two are indistinguishable. The output on the outside task looked as good as the output on the inside tasks. That's what makes the frontier dangerous: you don't feel yourself crossing it.

Two things happened in that experiment that nobody taught. Some consultants fell into a pattern the researchers called centaur: divide the work by task, give the tool what it's good at, keep the rest. Others worked as what they called cyborgs: weave in and out of the tool inside a single task, drafting, checking, redrafting. Both patterns emerged on their own, from consultants who had found the edge by working near it. The people who got hurt were the ones who never located the edge and treated the tool as uniformly reliable because it was uniformly fluent.

Here's the rule this book draws from it, and it's the practical content of Condition 4. Same-looking tasks can sit on opposite sides of the frontier. The only way to know which side you're on is to find the edge in your own domain, with your own tools, on your own work, and the weekly calibration loop is how you find it: one shipped decision, checked against what happened. Generic training can't do this for you. A course on "what AI is good at" freezes last quarter's map of a coastline that moves every quarter. By the time the curriculum is approved, the frontier has shifted, and the Drifter is the person still navigating by the old chart.

That study used a 2023 model. The specific tasks that sat outside the frontier then are inside it now, almost certainly. Which is the point. The location of the edge is perishable. The habit of checking for it isn't.

*

Which brings us to the system.

Part II has introduced each condition as though it operates independently: see yourself as the scarce input, embrace the effort, let your identity be clarified, calibrate continuously. That presentation was pedagogically necessary. You have to understand each part before the whole makes sense. But the claim of this book is that the conditions don't operate independently. They interact. They amplify each other. They form a system where the whole exceeds what any single condition could produce alone. That claim is a hypothesis, and this chapter will say so again before it ends. First, what it would look like if it's right.

The same product manager, the one with the weekly calibration loop. She's preparing a competitive analysis for quarterly planning. Her biggest competitor lost their head of engineering three weeks ago. She learned this at an industry conference, in a hallway conversation that isn't in any database, any news feed, any dataset an AI model has access to. She brings this intelligence into the collaboration: "The competitor's engineering leadership changed. Factor this into the roadmap stability assessment." That's Condition 1 operating. She's the scarce input. She's contributing what only she could know.

The AI generates an analysis. It's thorough, well-structured, and concludes that the competitor's product roadmap is stable. She pushes back: "Given the engineering leadership change, what scenarios would shift the roadmap? What historical patterns exist when companies lose technical leadership at this level?" The AI generates three scenarios she hadn't considered. One of them changes her strategic recommendation. That's Condition 2 operating. The effort of pushing back, of not accepting the first output, produced insight neither she nor the AI could have reached alone.

She doesn't feel diminished by any of this. Her sense of the situation is different: "My value is knowing what this intelligence means for this specific product in this specific market. AI handles the structured analysis. I handle the meaning." That's Condition 3 operating. Her identity is clarified as the person who understands context, relationships, and implications, not the one who assembles competitive data.

And then she notices the market sizing. AI's estimate seems high. Rather than accepting it or rejecting it wholesale, she checks: asks for sources, compares against internal data she has from last quarter's board report, identifies a methodological difference in how AI defines their addressable market versus how her company defines it. She adjusts her calibration: AI overestimates market size for their segment because it uses a broader definition. She'll weight it accordingly next time. That's Condition 4 operating. She's refining her model of where AI is reliable and where it needs correction.

All four conditions in one interaction. Each supporting the others.

*

Now watch what happens when one condition fails.

Same product manager. Same tools. Same expertise. But it's end of quarter, she's exhausted, the board deck is due tomorrow, and she needs this analysis done in thirty minutes instead of three hours.

She doesn't bring the competitor intelligence from the conference. It would require explaining context, providing background, adding nuance the AI would need to process the information correctly. She doesn't have time. Condition 1 collapses: her unique contribution stays in her head.

Because she didn't contribute anything distinctive, the AI's output is generic. But generic output doesn't trigger the impulse to push back, because there's nothing to push back against. It looks professional. It covers the standard categories. She accepts it. Condition 2 collapses: no effort, no cognitive engagement, no insight generation.

She feels vaguely resentful. A familiar thought surfaces: "Why am I even doing this if AI can just generate the analysis?" The resentment is Condition 3 under threat. When you're not bringing your expertise into the collaboration, the collaboration doesn't remind you of your value. It reminds you of your replaceability.

And she doesn't check the market sizing because she doesn't check anything. The output goes into the board deck as-is. Condition 4 collapses: no calibration, no refinement, no learning.

The output is competent. Professional. Indistinguishable from what any other product manager with the same subscription would produce. Her team uses it. Nobody notices what's missing. The board won't ask why the competitive analysis lacks the organizational intelligence that would have changed the strategic recommendation. They'll just make a slightly less informed decision and never know the counterfactual.

That's what low x looks like: invisible mediocrity, with no failure and no errors to point at, only the quiet absence of the human contribution, the competitor intelligence, the pushback, the calibration check, that would have made the output genuinely valuable.

*

The reinforcement loops are what would make this a system rather than a list.

When she brings the competitor intelligence (Condition 1 active), she has a reason to push back on the AI's conclusion. The AI said the roadmap is stable, but she knows something the AI doesn't. That knowledge creates the cognitive engagement Condition 2 requires. She can't just accept the output because she has evidence it's incomplete.

When she pushes back and gets better insight (Condition 2 active), she sees her value demonstrated in the output. The analysis is better because of what she contributed. That evidence reinforces her professional identity: her worth isn't in data assembly, it's in interpretation and judgment. Condition 3 strengthens.

When her identity isn't threatened (Condition 3 active), she can evaluate AI output honestly rather than defensively. She doesn't need AI to be wrong to feel valuable. She doesn't need it to be right to feel efficient. She can look at the market sizing with genuine curiosity: is this accurate or not? That emotional neutrality is what makes calibration possible. Condition 4 operates freely.

When she calibrates well (Condition 4 active), she knows where her judgment adds value and where it doesn't. That knowledge reinforces the sense of being the scarce input: not everywhere, not for everything, but specifically and demonstrably in the areas where her expertise matters most. Condition 1 strengthens.

The loop is self-sustaining. Remove any single condition and the loop degrades. Not catastrophically, not all at once, but in the gradual way the negative example illustrated: each missing condition makes the others harder to maintain.

*

This system claim isn't proven by any single study. Intellectual honesty requires saying that directly. No experiment has tested the four conditions as an interacting system. The claim is theoretical, built from converging evidence that each condition matters individually and from a consistent pattern in the literature: partial interventions produce partial results.

The pattern is worth naming precisely. The onboarding videos from Chapter 1, the ones almost nobody watched, were a Condition 1 adjacent intervention (building knowledge about your role with AI) attempted without addressing engagement, identity, or calibration. They produced nothing measurable. BCG's 2025 research showed that training increases AI usage but not impact: a Condition 1 adjacent success (adoption up) that fails to produce quality change because Conditions 2, 3, and 4 remain unaddressed. Gerlich's work on structured prompting showed that maintaining cognitive engagement (Condition 2) reduced offloading and improved reasoning, but the study didn't address identity or calibration. Improvement, but partial.

Three interventions, three different layers of the problem, three versions of the same shape: knowledge moves without behavior changing, behavior changes without quality changing, quality changes within a single condition while the rest of the system stays where it was. Each intervention proves its own logic and stops there. Which raises the next question almost on its own: what happens when an intervention reaches more than one condition at the same time?

The clinician study from earlier in this chapter answers it, even if the researchers didn't frame their workflow in H(x)AI terms. By requiring an independent diagnostic assessment before AI exposure, the structure simultaneously sustained cognitive engagement (Condition 2) and forced an act of calibration (Condition 4). Diagnostic accuracy improved. That is the closest thing to a comparison the literature currently offers, and it points the right direction.

The pattern is suggestive, not dispositive. One-condition interventions underperform. The one two-condition intervention shows promise. The prediction this framework makes: addressing three or four conditions simultaneously should produce disproportionate improvement. Not the sum of the individual effects. More than the sum. Because the conditions amplify each other.

That's a testable hypothesis. Stating it as a hypothesis rather than a finding is part of the book's intellectual commitment. The research testing this specific interaction effect hasn't been done. It should be. The prediction is on the table. What exists today is converging evidence and a structural logic that explains why the field's partial interventions keep producing the same disappointing results.

Chapter 4 borrowed the shape of this claim from Vroom, and the borrowing holds here with the same caveat: the multiplicative form is the structural precedent, motivation is a different dependent variable, and nothing Vroom showed about effort and reward counts as evidence for this system. What the form gives you is a way to see why tips don't work. A list of "five ways to collaborate better with AI" might touch one condition. None touches the system. And if the conditions amplify each other, a single condition operating without the others produces diminished returns. Not zero. Diminished. Which is what the partial-intervention data looks like: some improvement, never as much as expected, tending to decay back toward baseline. A training program that briefly activates Condition 1 (you see yourself as valuable) without addressing Condition 3 (but your identity still feels threatened) creates a tension that resolves toward the path of least resistance: back to the old pattern. The condition that wasn't addressed pulls the one that was back down.

*

This chapter closes Part II, and with it closes the theoretical argument the book has been building since the Introduction.

The arc: something is wrong with how humans collaborate with AI (Chapter 1). The current responses don't fix it because they work at the wrong layer (Chapter 2). The layer that matters is psychological: mental models, identity, the relationship between the human and the tool (Chapter 3). H(x)AI names the mechanism and gives it a structure: a multiplicative model where the mental model governs the coupling, deciding how much of the human's capability enters the collaboration and how much of the tool's capability the human draws out (Chapter 4). Four conditions move that multiplier toward productive collaboration: seeing yourself as the essential contributor (Chapter 5), embracing the greater effort productive collaboration demands (Chapter 6), allowing your professional identity to be clarified rather than threatened (Chapter 7), and calibrating continuously rather than trusting or distrusting by default (this chapter).

And those four conditions, the book argues, are a system, not a checklist. They reinforce each other. They degrade together. They would explain why partial interventions produce partial results and why the field's current approach keeps arriving at the same destination: usage up, impact flat, everyone puzzled about why.

Part III will show what this looks like when it's lived: for individuals, for organizations, and for the broader project of helping humanity get this relationship right. The theory is on the table. The question that remains is what changes when people actually internalize it.

But before leaving the theory, one observation about what the four conditions predict when they're operating.

The observable outcome isn't confidence. It isn't speed. It isn't a measurable "AI collaboration score." The outcome is something harder to quantify but unmistakable when you see it: intellectual flexibility. The willingness to bring genuine expertise and be changed by what you discover. To reject plausible-but-wrong output without anxiety. To accept genuinely valuable output without defensiveness. To make decisions and own them, knowing your calibration is good enough that the decision reflects your real judgment, not your fear or your ego.

Intellectual flexibility is a state, one that emerges when the four conditions are operating, and it's the thing that separates the one-in-five from everyone else. They aren't smarter, more experienced, or better trained. They can move — between trusting and questioning, between contributing and receiving, between holding a position and updating it — without the friction that locks most people into either surrender or fight.

That flexibility is what x looks like from the outside. It's what high-quality human-AI collaboration looks like when you're watching someone do it. And it's available to anyone willing to do the work the four conditions describe: the practice of seeing yourself clearly enough to bring your full capability into a collaboration with a tool that will never need you to, and being honest enough to keep checking whether you're right.

Notes

1. Recon Analytics survey data (2025), as reported by Directions on Microsoft, Windows Central, and Computerworld: 44% of lapsed Microsoft 365 Copilot users cited distrust of answers. See Chapter 1, Note 20 for the seat figures and dates.
2. Lee, D., Pruitt, J., Zhou, T., Du, J., & Odegaard, B. (2025). "Metacognitive sensitivity: The key to calibrating trust and optimal decision making with AI." *PNAS Nexus*, 4(5), pgaf133. DOI: 10.1093/pnasnexus/pgaf133.
3. Buçinca, Z., Malaya, M.B., & Gajos, K.Z. (2021). "To trust or to think: Cognitive forcing functions can reduce overreliance on AI in AI-assisted decision-making." *Proceedings of the ACM on Human-Computer Interaction*, 5(CSCW1), Article 188. DOI: 10.1145/3449287. arXiv:2102.09692. Three cognitive-forcing designs vs. two simple explainable-AI designs and a no-AI baseline; forcing designs substantially reduced overreliance; participants rated the most effective designs least favorably; benefits concentrated among participants with higher need for cognition.
4. Everett, S.S., et al. (2026). "From tool to teammate in a randomized controlled trial of clinician-AI collaborative workflows for diagnosis." *npj Digital Medicine*, 9, 409. DOI: 10.1038/s41746-026-02545-1. 70 clinicians. Independent diagnostic assessment before AI exposure improved accuracy over conventional resources. Full author list in Chapter 3, Note 1.
5. Dell'Acqua, F., McFowland, E. III, Mollick, E., Lifshitz-Assaf, H., Kellogg, K.C., Rajendran, S., Krayer, L., Candelon, F., & Lakhani, K.R. (2026). "Navigating the jagged technological frontier: Field experimental evidence of the effects of artificial intelligence on knowledge worker productivity and quality." *Organization Science*. DOI:

10.1287/orsc.2025.21838. Originally Harvard Business School Working Paper 24-013 (September 2023). 758 BCG consultants, 18 tasks, GPT-4 (fall 2023). Inside the frontier: +12.2% tasks completed, +25.1% speed, ~40% higher rated quality. Outside the frontier: 19 percentage points less likely to produce a correct answer. Centaur and cyborg work patterns emerged without instruction.

6. BCG (2025). "AI Adoption Puzzle: Why Usage Is Up but Impact Is Not." Workers with 5+ hours of training: 79% regular users vs. 67% with less training.

7. Gerlich, M. (2025). "From offloading to engagement: An experimental study on structured prompting and critical reasoning with generative AI." *Data*, 10(11), 172. DOI: 10.3390/data10110172. See Chapter 6, Note 4.

8. Vroom, V.H. (1964). *Work and Motivation*. John Wiley & Sons. See Chapter 4, Note 14.

PART III

Living It

CHAPTER 9

The Practitioner

Monday morning. A management consultant opens his laptop at 7:15, coffee still too hot to drink. He has a competitive analysis due by noon for a private equity client evaluating an acquisition target. He opens his AI tool and starts typing: not a request for a competitive analysis, but a brain dump. Everything he knows about this deal that the tool doesn't. The target company's CEO gave a conference keynote six weeks ago where he mentioned supply chain problems without being asked. The PE firm's operating partner has a track record of gutting R&D budgets post-acquisition, which means the target's product pipeline is more vulnerable than the financials suggest. Two board members are approaching mandatory retirement age, and the replacement bench is thin.

He feeds all of this into the collaboration. Then he asks the AI to challenge his assumptions about the target's competitive moat. It pushes back on his assessment of the supply chain risk, pointing to recent capital expenditure data he hadn't pulled. He considers it, decides the capex spending is cosmetic based on where the money actually went (facilities, not logistics infrastructure), and tells the AI why. The analysis sharpens. By 10:30, he has a deliverable that no other consultant working this deal could have produced, because no other consultant had that combination of intelligence, judgment, and willingness to argue with a machine, at nine on a Monday morning, about where the money went.

Friday afternoon. Same consultant, same laptop, same AI subscription. Different week, different client, but structurally the same task: a market entry assessment for a consumer goods company considering a new category. He's tired. The week has been long. He types: "Create a market entry analysis for a mid-size consumer goods company entering the premium pet food category." The AI produces something clean, organized, and completely generic. He reads it, fixes two formatting issues, and sends it. The analysis could have come from any consultant at any firm with the same subscription. It probably has.

Same person. Same tools. Same professional expertise sitting in the same head. On Monday, that expertise entered the collaboration. On Friday, it didn't. The two deliverables differ in kind.

*

This is what x looks like in practice. Not a personality type. Not a skill level. A state that shifts within the same person, sometimes within the same day, depending on whether the conditions are operating or whether they've gone quiet.

The theory chapters described x as the mental model multiplier: the set of assumptions, beliefs, and psychological dispositions that determine how much of a person's actual capability enters the collaboration with AI, and how much of the tool's the person draws out. In those chapters, x was a construct. Here, it becomes visible. Because in daily practice, the difference between high x and low x isn't abstract. It's the difference between work that could only come from you and work that could come from anyone.

The observable behaviors aren't mysterious, and Chapter 4 said what they are: the marks you can check before you know how the work turned out. When x is high, a person contributes context the tool couldn't have had before asking it to generate anything. They form a view before they open it. They push back on outputs that don't match their domain knowledge and reject something specific rather than the whole. They catch errors that only someone with their experience would notice. They go back and retest a task they once decided the tool couldn't do. They treat AI suggestions as starting points for their own thinking, not endpoints.

When x is low, the same person types a request, reviews the output for obvious problems, cleans up the formatting, and moves on. The interaction is efficient. The output is competent. And the thing that makes their work distinctive, the accumulated expertise that took years to build, stays locked inside their head while the AI produces something any subscriber could have gotten.

The research is consistent with this pattern. The meta-analysis Chapter 1 told found the gains where the human had real capability to bring and brought it into creation work; the Monday consultant is that case, and the Friday consultant is the same person with the same capability, unbrought. The Wharton students from the same chapter kept what they'd learned only when the tool made them think first; Monday is the scaffolded condition, Friday is the unscaffolded one. The studies measured the aggregate. The Monday-Friday illustration shows what the aggregate feels like from the inside.

Which means x isn't something you have or don't have. It's something you're doing or not doing, in this interaction, with this tool, on this task. That's both the good news and the bad news. Good, because it means improvement doesn't require a personality overhaul or a certification program. Bad, because it means the conditions have to be maintained actively. They don't install once and run forever. They fluctuate with energy, attention, time pressure, and the thousand small decisions that determine whether you bring yourself to the work or let the tool carry it.

*

The four conditions described in the previous chapters (seeing yourself as the essential contributor, expecting the collaboration to demand real effort, understanding your identity as clarified rather than threatened, and maintaining ongoing calibration) don't fail one at a time in neat isolation. In practice, they tend to collapse into recognizable patterns. They're tendencies, not types or diagnoses, that most people fall into at different times, depending on which condition has gone quiet. Think of them as a flashlight, not a label: they help you see which pattern you're in right now, not which kind of person you are.

The scenarios that follow are composites, built from common patterns across industries and roles. They're illustrations of how the conditions operate in practice, not case studies of specific individuals. The dynamics are real in the sense that practitioners across many fields will recognize them. They're not evidence for H(x)AI. The evidence lives in the research chapters. These are demonstrations of what the theory looks like when it shows up at someone's desk.

*

The first pattern: the Deferrer.

A mid-career project manager, twelve years of experience, has become the most efficient person on her team since adopting AI tools. She produces project plans in half the time. Her stakeholder communications are polished and professional. Her risk registers cover every category the methodology calls for. Her manager is thrilled with the output volume.

Here's what her manager doesn't see. Before AI, her project plans included a section she called "the political map": an informal assessment of which stakeholders were aligned, which were in conflict, and which relationships would determine whether the project actually got resources or died in committee. She knew, for instance, that the VP of Engineering and the VP of Product hadn't spoken directly in six months, that all communication routed through a director who softened every message, and that any deliverable requiring joint sign-off from both VPs would stall unless she brokered the conversation herself. None of this lived in any document. It lived in twelve years of reading rooms.

She stopped including the political map. Not deliberately. AI couldn't generate it, so it didn't appear in the first draft, and she stopped adding it because the first draft looked complete without it. Technically competent, and politically naive. Three of her last four projects have stalled at the approval stage. She attributes this to "organizational dysfunction." She's half right: the dysfunction is real. But she used to navigate it, and now she doesn't, because the part of her expertise that navigated it has been quietly edited out of her workflow.

The Deferrer's signature is a contribution that's genuine and irreplaceable, withheld because the person doesn't recognize it as expertise. "AI has more data than I do" is the Deferrer's refrain. It's true in a narrow sense: AI has access to more information. But information and judgment are different things. The project manager's knowledge of who talks to whom and what it means for resource allocation isn't data. It's intelligence, in the strategic sense, and no AI tool can generate it because no AI tool sat in those meetings, read those facial expressions, or noticed which emails got answered in minutes and which got answered in days.

The Deferrer isn't lazy. The Deferrer has a self-efficacy problem dressed as efficiency. Condition 1 has gone quiet: the belief that the human is the essential contributor has been replaced by the belief that AI is the capable one and the human's job is to review and approve. The perceived-control drop that Wu and colleagues measured, told in Chapter 5, is the mechanism: people didn't just lose confidence in their output when AI entered the workflow. They lost the sense that they were the agent in the interaction. The Deferrer is living that finding.

*

The second pattern: the Coaster.

A content strategist at a B2B software company produces a weekly blog post, three social threads, and a monthly newsletter. Before AI, this took most of his week. Now it takes a day and a half. He reads each piece before publishing. They sound professional. The grammar is clean. The structure is logical.

What he's stopped noticing is the drift. Six months ago, the blog posts reflected his understanding of the company's specific market position: a mid-market player competing on implementation speed against enterprise incumbents. The posts named specific competitor weaknesses, referenced customer conversations he'd had, and made arguments grounded in the company's actual differentiation. The current posts are about "the importance of digital transformation" and "why customer experience matters in B2B." They could run on any company's blog in any industry. The voice has flattened into a register that sounds professional and says nothing.

The decline was gradual enough to be invisible. No single post was the moment quality dropped. Each one was marginally less specific than the last, and each one looked fine in isolation. The fluency trap is fully engaged: the output passes every surface-level quality check because AI is excellent at producing text that reads well. The checks that would catch the drift, the ones that ask "does this reflect what we actually know about our market?" and "would a competitor's content strategist have written the same thing?", require the kind of active engagement that Condition 2 describes. The Coaster has stopped performing those checks because the output doesn't trigger the alarm that something is wrong.

The Coaster's signature is ease. The work feels frictionless, which is the diagnostic signal the Coaster is missing. Condition 2 says productive AI collaboration should feel harder, not easier, because the effort of pushing back, questioning, and redirecting is the multiplier in action. When the effort disappears, so does the multiplier. The Coaster isn't disengaged by choice. The Coaster is efficient, responsive, and meeting every deadline. The trap is that efficiency and disengagement feel identical from the inside. The Coaster is Gerlich's unguided condition from Chapter 6, playing out at a content desk: output volume up, cognitive engagement down, quality silently degrading beneath a surface that looks fine.

*

The third pattern: the Defender.

A senior litigation partner at a two-hundred-person law firm has been practicing for twenty-three years. He'll use AI for document review ("that's volume work"), for summarizing depositions ("mechanical"), and for drafting standard motions ("template stuff"). He won't let it near case strategy. "I didn't get where I am by trusting machines with the work that matters."

He's right about one thing: his strategic judgment is genuinely valuable. Twenty-three years of reading judges, anticipating opposing counsel's moves, and knowing which arguments land in which courtrooms has produced pattern recognition that no AI currently matches. His win rate reflects real expertise. The Defender's expertise isn't imaginary.

What the Defender can't see, what no Defender can see, is the cost of the boundary he's drawn. He'll never discover the cases AI would have flagged in the deposition summaries that he skimmed instead of reading closely. He'll never see the pattern in opposing counsel's filing history across twelve cases that data analysis could have surfaced in minutes. He'll never know about the judge's unusual ruling in an obscure jurisdiction that's directly relevant to his current argument because he doesn't ask AI to look where he wouldn't think to look. The Defender's expertise is real. His blind spots are also real, and his refusal to let AI into strategic territory means the blind spots stay permanent.

The Defender's signature is a selective boundary that maps exactly to identity. The mechanical work (document review, summarization, drafting) doesn't threaten his sense of professional worth, so AI is welcome there. The strategic work (case theory, argument selection, courtroom tactics) is where his identity lives, and admitting AI could contribute to that space feels like admitting that twenty-three years of experience aren't sufficient. Condition 3 describes the resolution: professional identity clarified rather than threatened. The Defender hasn't reached it because he's protecting the mechanical components of his expertise (I'm the one who builds the strategy) instead of recognizing the judgment underneath (I'm the one who knows what the strategy should accomplish and why). Chapter 7 told the research that explains the intensity: identity threat operates as its own barrier, independent of how much someone knows about AI and separate from resistance to change in general. The Defender isn't resisting because he doesn't understand AI. He's resisting because the specific territory AI wants to enter is the territory where his professional self lives. That's not irrational. It's protective. And it's costly, because the protection prevents exactly the kind of augmentation that would make his genuine expertise more powerful.

One honesty note, because it matters here more than anywhere. The scope Chapters 5 through 7 stated applies to the Defender in full: his work has a deep judgment layer, and the clarification Condition 3 describes is available to him. The framework doesn't promise that every professional role has a hidden judgment layer waiting to be revealed, and this chapter won't either. The Defender's situation is specific: he has real expertise that AI can't replicate, and he's preventing it from amplifying what he already does well. That's the version of the pattern this chapter addresses.

*

The fourth pattern: the Drifter.

The data scientist from Chapter 8 is the Drifter, and her story is worth one more pass now that the pattern has a name. She evaluated AI coding tools when they first became available for statistical modeling and ran her own tests: gave the tools a series of modeling tasks she'd previously completed, compared the outputs to her own work. The tools made errors in specification that would have produced misleading results in production. She concluded, reasonably, that AI tools weren't reliable for the kind of statistical work she did, and she stopped using them for that purpose. That assessment was accurate. In 2024.

Eighteen months later, the tools have improved substantially for exactly the kind of statistical modeling she tested. A junior colleague who started using the updated tools is producing valid models faster than she is. She doesn't know this because she never rechecked. Her calibration is frozen eighteen months in the past while the tools moved on.

The Drifter's signature is an outdated model that was once accurate. The Drifter isn't resistant. She made a reasonable assessment based on real evidence. The problem is that calibration has a shelf life. AI capabilities change on a timeline measured in months, not years. A reasonable judgment from one year becomes an outdated assumption the next, and without active recalibration, there's no mechanism for the Drifter to discover the gap between her model and reality. Condition 4 describes calibration as a continuous practice; the Drifter skipped the "continuous" part. Lee and colleagues' distinction from Chapter 8 is the one that applies: the question was never whether she trusted the tool, but whether her confidence still tracked its accuracy. In 2024 it did. It doesn't now, and she can't tell, because the miscalibration is invisible without active checking.

*

Most people aren't purely one pattern. A person can defer in one domain (letting AI handle financial modeling because "it has more data") while defending in another (refusing to let AI near client communications because "that's my voice"). The same person might coast through routine tasks on Tuesday and engage deeply with a high-stakes project on Wednesday. The patterns overlap, shift, and combine.

That's actually the point. They're diagnostic signals, not categories. The value isn't in labeling yourself as "a Deferrer" or "a Defender."

The value is in recognizing which pattern you're falling into right now, in this collaboration, with this tool, on this task. The patterns are a flashlight, not a label: they illuminate what's happening in the moment, not what kind of person you are.

The Barnum effect (the tendency for people to accept vague personality descriptions as uniquely applying to them) is a real risk with any typology. If you read all four patterns and thought "that's me" for each one, that's the Barnum effect operating. The antidote is specificity. Don't ask "which type am I?" Ask: "In the last AI interaction I had, which condition was weakest? Did I bring my genuine expertise, or did I defer? Would Chapter 5's commodity test have caught me? Did the work feel appropriately hard, or suspiciously easy? Did I protect a boundary that serves my identity more than my output? Is my assessment of what this tool can and can't do current?"

Those questions are more useful than any classification because they point to action. If you deferred, bring more of what you know next time. If you coasted, make the next interaction harder on purpose. If you defended, try letting AI into one corner of the protected territory and see what happens. If you drifted, spend ten minutes testing the tool on something you haven't tried in six months. The diagnostic is only useful if it changes what you do tomorrow.

*

So here is what Tuesday can look like. Not a method. The book has argued against methods for eight chapters and isn't going to hand you one now. What follows is the smallest set of habits that keep the four conditions alive under ordinary pressure, and each of them is something you can do on one task this week.

The first habit is a sorting question you ask before you open the tool, and it has three answers. Some work doesn't need your judgment at all: meeting notes, formatting, a first pass at facts that are public and checkable. Delegate that, fully, and don't feel bad about it. Some work is judgment work, the kind the scope in Chapter 5 described, where you bring context the tool can't have and you expect to push back. Collaborate on that, which means you go in with a view and you leave having changed it or defended it. And some work should not go to the tool at all: the tool is wrong for the task, the data you'd feed it is bad, or a fluent error would cost more than you can verify against. Refuse that, and refuse it as a calibrated decision rather than a mood. The reason the sorting matters is that the Introduction's word "surrender" is easy to mishear. Surrender is abdicated judgment: you had a call to make and let the output make it. Delegation is allocated judgment: you made the call that this task didn't need one. The first collapses the collaboration. The second is how a professional spends a Tuesday. "Don't surrender" has never meant "fight everything," and the Defender is what happens when someone hears it that way.

The second habit is the commodity test, which Chapter 5 introduced and which belongs here because it's the one check you can run before the work is done. If any other subscriber with the same tool would have gotten the same output from what you typed, your scarce input didn't enter. That's it. Run it on the prompt, not the result, because the result will look fine either way; that's the fluency trap. Chapter 4 listed the marks that pass the test: context that isn't public, a view you held before you opened the tool, something specific you rejected. If none of them are present in what you sent, the Deferrer or the Coaster is at the keyboard, and you know which one by whether the work felt like nothing or felt like relief.

The third habit is the weekly calibration loop, which Chapter 8 named, and it is Condition 4 made concrete, because "ask yourself if you're over-trusting" is not a practice and never becomes one. Ten minutes, once a week, one decision that shipped. Write down the task. Write down what you expected the tool to do on it. Write down what it actually did. Write down what you caught, and, if you're honest, what you didn't. Then write down what you'll trust next time and what you won't. Five lines. The log is not for anyone else.

Its whole purpose is that, after ten weeks, you have fifty lines that describe where the frontier runs in your own work, with your own tools, on your own tasks, and no course or vendor can give you that map because it isn't theirs. The data scientist in the Drifter pattern is what a person looks like without this habit: accurate once, and never again.

The fourth habit is for diagnosis-shaped work, and it comes straight from the clinicians in Chapter 3. Any time the task is "what's wrong here," "which of these," or "what should we do," write your own answer before you look at the tool's. One sentence is enough. The physicians who did this diagnosed more accurately than the ones who worked with conventional resources, and the reason is the anchoring problem Chapter 8 described: once the fluent answer is on the screen, you are editing it, not judging it. Think first, and you have something to compare against. Skip it, and you have a first draft you didn't write and will probably keep. Chapter 8's jagged frontier is the other reason this habit earns its ten seconds: the tasks where the tool is confidently wrong look exactly like the tasks where it's confidently right, and your prior answer is the only instrument you carry that can tell them apart.

That's the whole practice layer. Sort the task, test the prompt, log one decision a week, think before you look. None of it takes an hour. All of it is easier to skip on a Friday afternoon than to do, which is why the Friday consultant exists.

*

One last illustration, and a label before I describe it.

What follows is one practitioner's worked example. A single person, the one who built the framework, checking his own practice against the four conditions the way the rest of this chapter has asked you to check yours. It is not evidence for H(x)AI. The evidence lives in the research: the meta-analysis, the Wharton trial, the developer productivity data, the identity-threat findings, the metacognitive sensitivity work. Those studies have sample sizes, controls, and peer review. My practice has none of that. What it can do is show what reading the four conditions as a diagnostic mirror looks like in someone's working week, including a person who has every motive to want the framework to work.

I use AI every day. Some days my practice looks like the Monday consultant from the opening of this chapter. Some days it looks like the Friday consultant. The difference is not stable, not heroic, and not always visible to me in the moment. So I read the conditions back against the work and check what I find.

Condition 1: was I the scarce input? On the Monday-shaped days, the answer is yes. I started with what I know about the client, the situation, the constraint that doesn't appear in any public document, and the AI's job was to challenge and extend that. On the Friday-shaped days, I typed a generic prompt and accepted what came back. The mirror catches the difference. The work product confirms it.

Condition 2: did the collaboration demand more, not less? The interactions I am proud of took effort. I argued with the AI. I rejected outputs that felt too smooth for the difficulty of the problem. The interactions I am embarrassed by took almost nothing. The output looked clean. The time was short. The cost was invisible until I read it later.

Condition 3: did my professional identity stay clarified rather than threatened? On the good days, the parts of the work I am actually hired to do, the framing of the problem, the judgment about which question matters, the choice of where to push back, are still mine, and the AI handles the mechanical layer underneath. On the bad days, I am either deferring on judgment that should be mine, or guarding territory the AI was never trying to take. Both signal an identity question I haven't resolved on that day, on that task.

Condition 4: am I checking my calibration, or trusting last quarter's read of the tools? This is the condition I miss most often. The tools change. My sense of what they can and can't do drifts. The mirror catches it only when I deliberately look, which means it stops catching anything the moment I stop looking.

That is the worked example. One person, self-reporting, with the framework he built operating as both the mirror and the practice it reflects. Survivorship bias, confirmation bias, and the simple fact that I am motivated to believe the framework works all mean my own experience isn't evidence. I can't compare my AI-assisted output to what I would have produced without AI, or what I would have produced with the same tools but a different mental model. The developers in Chapter 1 believed they were faster while the clock said slower, in early 2025, and the researchers who measured it have since said the tools moved on while the misjudgment didn't. That finding should make any practitioner cautious about their own self-report. Mine included.

So take it for what it is. One practitioner's worked example, offered not as proof but as a record of what reading the four conditions as a mirror looks like in practice. If the conditions are sound, they should be demonstrable by anyone who internalizes them, not just by the person who named them.

*

What changes when the conditions are operating isn't dramatic in the moment. There's no epiphany, no transformation, no before-and-after montage. The change is in the texture of the work. A person operating with high x makes different micro-decisions throughout a collaboration: contributing context before asking the AI to generate, noticing when an output feels too smooth for the complexity of the problem, pushing back on a recommendation that doesn't match their domain knowledge, checking whether their trust in the tool's answer is warranted or habitual.

Each of those micro-decisions is small. None of them is heroic. Together, they're the difference between work that could only come from this person and work that could come from anyone with the same subscription. That difference shows up in client feedback. It shows up in colleague respect. It shows up in the practitioner's own relationship to their work: the sense that the work is still yours, that your expertise still matters, that the collaboration is making you more effective rather than making you — the word nobody wants to say — redundant.

The Monday consultant and the Friday consultant are the same person, with the same knowledge, talent, and tools. What differed was whether the conditions were active or dormant. So the question worth carrying out of this chapter is what it takes to keep them alive when everything, fatigue, deadlines, the ease of accepting the first output, is working to put them to sleep.

The next chapter takes that question from individual practice to organizational context. Because the conditions don't operate in a vacuum. They operate inside teams, cultures, and incentive structures that either support them or systematically undermine them. The consultant who brings his full expertise on Monday might stop doing it if his firm rewards volume over insight, if his peers penalize him for using AI at all, or if the organizational culture treats speed as the only metric that matters.

The conditions are personal. The environment that sustains or kills them is structural. That's the subject of Chapter 10.

Notes

1. Vaccaro, M., Almaatouq, A., & Malone, T. (2024). "When combinations of humans and AI are useful: A systematic review and meta-analysis." *Nature Human Behaviour*, 8(12), 2293-2303. DOI: 10.1038/s41562-024-02024-1. See Chapter 1, Note 1.

2. Bastani, H., Bastani, O., Sungu, A., Ge, H., Kabakcı, Ö., & Mariman, R. (2025). "Generative AI without guardrails can harm learning: Evidence from high school mathematics." *Proceedings of the National Academy of Sciences*, 122(26), e2422633122. See Chapter 1, Note 12.

3. Wu, S., Liu, Y., Ruan, M., Chen, S., & Xie, X.-Y. (2025). "Human-generative AI collaboration enhances task performance but undermines human's intrinsic motivation." *Scientific Reports*, 15, 15105. DOI: 10.1038/s41598-025-98385-2. See Chapter 5, Note 4.

4. Gerlich, M. (2025). "From offloading to engagement: An experimental study on structured prompting and critical reasoning with generative AI." *Data*, 10(11), 172. DOI: 10.3390/data10110172. See Chapter 6, Note 4.

5. Mirbabaie, M., Brünker, F., Möllmann Frick, N.R.J., & Stieglitz, S. (2022). "The rise of artificial intelligence – understanding the AI identity threat at the workplace." *Electronic Markets*, 32(1), 73-99. DOI: 10.1007/s12525-021-00496-x. See Chapter 7, Note 1.

6. Lee, D., Pruitt, J., Zhou, T., Du, J., & Odegaard, B. (2025). "Metacognitive sensitivity: The key to calibrating trust and optimal decision making with AI." *PNAS Nexus*, 4(5), pgaf133. DOI: 10.1093/pnasnexus/pgaf133. See Chapter 8, Note 2.

7. Everett, S.S., et al. (2026). "From tool to teammate in a randomized controlled trial of clinician-AI collaborative workflows for diagnosis." *npj Digital Medicine*, 9, 409. DOI: 10.1038/s41746-026-02545-1. See Chapter 3, Note 1.

8. Becker, J., Rush, N., Barnes, B., & Rein, D. (2025). "Measuring the impact of early-2025 AI on experienced open-source developer productivity." METR. arXiv:2507.09089. See also Becker et al. (2026), METR, February 24, 2026, https://metr.org/blog/2026-02-24-uplift-update/. See Chapter 1, Notes 6–7.

CHAPTER 10

The Organization

The consulting firm from Chapter 1, nine months on. The head of digital transformation has a slide deck that would make any CEO smile: 82 percent weekly active usage, 91 percent training completion, employee satisfaction with the AI tools at 4.1 out of 5, time-to-first-draft down 40 percent across the strategy team. Every KPI green.

He presents it to the leadership team on a Tuesday morning. The COO nods. The CFO asks about the ROI calculation. The CEO says, "This is exactly what we needed to see."

Then the chief client officer, who has been quiet, does what the managing partner did in Chapter 1, in front of the whole room this time. Three proposals from before, three from after, a paragraph from each, read aloud. The room goes still. Cleaner. Faster. Interchangeable. The strategic specificity that clients were paying a premium for had been quietly edited out, and not by the tool.

Every metric on the transformation leader's slide was accurate. And every metric measured the wrong thing.

*

This is the organizational version of the gap Chapter 1 described at the individual level. But it operates differently at scale, and the difference matters. When one person operates at a low x, bringing little of their genuine expertise into AI collaboration, the cost is one person's unrealized potential. When most of an organization operates at low x, the cost multiplies across every client engagement, every product decision, every strategic analysis the company produces. The tool investment doesn't fail. It succeeds at producing more of something nobody needed: generic, interchangeable output at enterprise volume.

The stakes scale the way Chapter 4's argument did, and with the same honesty: x doesn't come with instrumentation, and an organization doesn't have an average you could read off a dashboard. What the model says is that the same people, with the same tools, bringing much more of what they already know into the work, produce something categorically different from what they produce now. Not incrementally better. Different in kind, the way the second architect's building was different from the first's. That is the CEO-level argument, and it has nothing to do with software procurement.

The surveys say the current state is the norm, not the exception, and they should be read as surveys.

Writer's 2026 enterprise report found 79 percent of organizations reporting significant AI adoption challenges, a higher share than the year before. Fifty-four percent of the C-suite executives surveyed agreed that AI adoption is "tearing their company apart," which is survey language, not a clinical finding, and it's still a striking thing for half of a boardroom to endorse. BCG's 2025 analysis put the same shape in four words: usage is up, impact is not. Their AI at Work survey found 85 percent of leaders regularly using AI against 51 percent of frontline employees, a gap they called the "silicon ceiling." But the more important ceiling isn't between users and non-users. It's between usage and value. Organizations reporting the highest adoption rates aren't reporting corresponding improvements in output quality, client satisfaction, or competitive differentiation. They've closed the adoption gap. The collaboration quality gap remains wide open.

Look again at that leader-frontline gap. It's two groups inside the same company forming different beliefs about the same tool, and the usage numbers are only the visible part. The people using AI daily develop a working sense of what it's good for and where it fails them. The people who aren't, watching from outside while leadership talks about efficiency gains, form a different picture from the same announcements. Both pictures are rational given what each group has actually experienced, and that's the point: the fracture isn't about information. Everyone got the same memo. It's about experience. Mental models get built by doing, and a group that hasn't done anything with the tool builds its model out of whatever else is available. In a year of efficiency announcements, what's available is not reassuring.

Be careful about what this chapter is claiming. Organizations fail at AI for reasons that have nothing to do with anyone's mental model: bad data, incentives that reward volume, use cases chosen because they demoed well, tools bought before anyone wrote down what "working" would mean. Those are real, they're common, and the four conditions don't fix them. What the four conditions name is an underrecognized constraint that shows up once the tools are deployed and the other problems are handled: whether the environment lets people bring what they know. That's the layer this chapter is about, and it's a layer the adoption dashboards don't see. Adoption metrics are to collaboration quality what a bathroom scale is to cardiovascular health: they measure something real, and it's the wrong thing.

*

The most common organizational response to the collaboration quality gap is mandates. If people aren't getting value from AI, require them to use it more. Measure compliance. Tie it to performance reviews. The logic feels obvious: if the bottleneck is how people collaborate, push them to collaborate more.

Klarna, which Chapter 4 told, is the limiting case: an organization that optimized cost per interaction, took the human term to zero for the interactions it automated, and by its CEO's own account got lower quality and had to bring humans back. That's what a multiplicative relationship does when a term hits zero, and it isn't a story about mandates. But you don't have to go to Klarna's extreme to see the mandate problem. Most organizations mandate use, not replacement: require employees to incorporate AI into workflows, track adoption metrics, report compliance. Remember the onboarding videos from Chapter 1, the ones almost nobody watched. Not because people are lazy. Because they correctly sensed that watching someone explain AI wouldn't change anything that mattered.

The mandate produces exactly what mandates always produce: compliance without engagement. Employees use the tool because they're told to. They type requests and accept outputs because that satisfies the metric. The organization's dashboard shows adoption climbing. The work product stays flat. This is the specific failure mode the multiplicative model predicts: widespread adoption with minimal collaboration quality. Usage goes up. x doesn't move.

Right? Everyone who's led an AI rollout recognizes this. The team meeting where the manager asks "is everyone using the tools?" and twenty heads nod, and then you look at the actual output and it's the same work product with slightly better formatting. The compliance is real. The collaboration isn't.

The perceived-control finding from Chapter 5 is the mechanism, and it should intensify under mandate conditions. Self-determination theory, one of the most validated frameworks in motivational psychology, identifies autonomy as a precondition for genuine engagement. Mandates remove autonomy by definition. The person using AI because they chose to bring something to the collaboration carries a fundamentally different quality of attention than the person using AI because their manager checks the dashboard on Friday.

Here's the thing about mandates. They can produce adoption; that is what they're for. They cannot produce the four conditions. You can't order someone to believe their expertise matters when they sit down with the tool. You can't order someone to push back on AI output rather than accepting it. You can't order someone to resolve the identity threat that makes them hide their AI use from colleagues. You can't order someone to maintain an accurate, updated model of what AI can and can't do in their domain. Those are psychological states. They require conditions, not commands.

So if mandates don't work, what does?

*

The answer starts with infrastructure most organizations don't recognize as infrastructure.

Reif, Larrick, and Soll published a finding in 2025 that should reshape how every organization thinks about AI deployment. Across four preregistered experiments with over four thousand participants, they measured the social cost of using AI at work: a 9 percent reduction in how peers rate your competence. For women in engineering, the penalty is 13 percent. When male non-adopters evaluate female engineers who use AI, the penalty reaches 26 percent.

Those numbers mean that in the professional environments the study modeled, the social cost of using AI is real and measurable: the environment punishes the people who are trying to collaborate productively.

Think about what that does to the conditions over time.

Condition 1 says you're the scarce input, that your expertise is what makes the collaboration valuable. But if demonstrating deep AI engagement costs you competence ratings, why would you demonstrate it publicly? Condition 2 says productive collaboration demands more cognitive effort, not less. But if that effort is visible and the social cost is real, the rational move is to minimize visible engagement. Condition 3 says your professional identity is clarified, not threatened, by AI. But the competence penalty makes the threat concrete: your peers literally think less of you for using the tool. Condition 4 says calibration requires admitting when you were wrong about AI's capabilities. But admitting miscalibration in a penalizing environment means admitting you relied on something that your peers already think makes you look weak.

The competence penalty doesn't just discourage AI use. It works against every condition required for productive collaboration.

Picture two developers on the same engineering team. Both use AI extensively. Both bring genuine architecture expertise into the interaction. Both push back on generated code and catch subtle design errors. Both produce better work because of how they collaborate with the tool. In peer reviews, both receive lower competence ratings than colleagues who write everything by hand. Within three months, both stop using AI for anything visible to their peers. They still use it privately, on tasks nobody will see. The organizational environment hasn't changed their capability. It's changed their willingness to exercise it where it matters.

Now notice the gender dimension. One of those developers is a woman. Her competence penalty is 13 percent at baseline, potentially 26 percent from male non-adopting peers. She stops using AI faster and more completely than her male colleague. Not because she's less capable or more risk-averse, but because the cost is structurally higher for her. The organization loses its most productive AI collaboration from the person paying the highest price for it. This is structural. Organizations that don't address the competence penalty create environments where women face steeper costs for productive AI engagement, which compounds existing disparities in who benefits from AI tools.

This is why psychological safety isn't aspirational for AI adoption. It's infrastructure. The concept belongs to Amy Edmondson, whose research over two decades established that psychological safety, the shared belief that a team is safe for interpersonal risk-taking, is among the strongest predictors of team learning and effectiveness.

Google's Project Aristotle found the same thing across 180 of its own teams. The insight is well established. What the competence penalty data adds is the AI-specific mechanism: a measured social cost that functions as an environmental suppressor of every condition productive AI collaboration requires.

The practical difference between an unsafe environment and a safe one shows up at the team level. Same company as the two developers, different team, different manager. This manager opens meetings by sharing her own AI experiments, including the ones that produced garbage. She frames AI collaboration as a skill the team is developing together, not a shortcut that signals weakness. She says, explicitly: "Using AI well, bringing your judgment to it, pushing back when it's wrong, that's what expertise looks like now." The competence penalty doesn't disappear. But the local environment counteracts it. Developers on this team use AI openly, share what works and what doesn't, and their collaboration is visibly better than on the team where AI use is a quiet, private secret.

Safety doesn't directly increase x. It removes the environmental suppression that keeps x low. Employees who have genuinely internalized the conditions, who believe their expertise matters, who have developed a calibrated model of AI's strengths and failures in their domain, will still suppress all of it if the environment punishes the behavior the conditions enable. Safety is necessary. Not sufficient. Without it, every other intervention degrades.

The CEO who has already invested in psychological safety may find this argument validates what they're doing rather than adding something new. Good. That means the infrastructure is in place. What they may not have done is connected it explicitly to AI collaboration, and the competence penalty data shows why that connection matters: the social cost of AI use is specific enough, measured enough, and gendered enough to require direct attention even in organizations that consider themselves psychologically safe in general.

*

The second piece of organizational infrastructure is less obvious but equally important: how people encounter the conditions in the first place.

The dominant model is training-first. Teach people about AI, then send them to use it. The assumption is that knowledge precedes productive behavior. The evidence says otherwise. And the most compelling evidence comes from people who were never trained at all.

The BCG field experiment Chapter 8 told, 758 consultants on eighteen realistic tasks, one of the largest field experiments on AI and professional work, didn't teach anyone how to collaborate with AI. It gave them access and observed what happened. Two distinct collaboration patterns emerged on their own. Some consultants became what the researchers called "centaurs": they analyzed the problem themselves, identified which subtasks AI could handle (data synthesis, comparable case research, initial framework generation), delegated those, and focused their own effort on strategic interpretation, client-specific judgment, and recommendation design. Others became "cyborgs": constant back-and-forth, using AI as a sparring partner on the same subtask, challenging and being challenged in rapid iteration. Nobody taught either pattern. Both emerged from doing real work. Both produced superior results inside the frontier, and Chapter 8 already said what happened outside it.

That jagged frontier is why training-first fails at the organizational level. A training program designed in January teaches people where the frontier was in January. By March, the model has updated and the frontier has moved. The consultant who memorized which tasks to delegate and which to keep is working from an outdated map. The consultant who has tested AI on fifty real client engagements knows the frontier empirically, in her specific domain, with her specific tools. Her map updates because her practice updates.

The centaurs discovered Condition 1 through practice: they learned which parts of the task required their scarce input by experiencing what happened when they withheld it. The cyborgs discovered Condition 2 the same way: the constant engagement naturally maintained cognitive effort because the back-and-forth demanded it. Both groups discovered calibration empirically. They learned where AI excels and where it fails not from a workshop but from the work itself.

A meta-analysis by Thomann and Deutscher supports the principle across contexts. Sixty-eight studies, consistent finding: digital scaffolding that maintains learner engagement significantly enhances achievement. The effect size is moderate, not dramatic. The consistency is the point. Structured experience that keeps people cognitively engaged outperforms passive information delivery everywhere it's been tested.

But "experience-first" doesn't mean "figure it out yourself." That distinction matters, because it's where this argument is most vulnerable to misreading, and the misreading has a name in the learning literature. Kirschner, Sweller, and Clark made the case in 2006 that minimally guided instruction, the "discover it yourself" model, reliably underperforms guided instruction, because novices without structure don't know what to attend to. Their argument is against unguided discovery, and it's the right argument. The Wharton experiment from Chapter 1 tested both versions in miniature: unrestricted access, experience without structure, left students below their baseline; the scaffolded tutor, experience with structure, built capability that stayed. Both were experience-first. Only one was structured. The structure made the difference, and "experience-first" in this book always means the structured kind.

For organizations, the design principle follows directly: stop building AI training programs. Start designing AI collaboration experiences. The difference isn't semantic. A training program says "here are ten ways to use AI effectively" and delivers through workshops, videos, and learning modules. It measures completion and knowledge retention. An experience design says "here is a real task from your domain, work with AI to complete it, bring your expertise, push back when the output doesn't match what you know, notice where AI adds value and where it doesn't." It measures whether the person's collaboration pattern changed. Whether they brought more expertise. Whether they calibrated.

The experience design has a structural advantage the training program can't match: it touches all four conditions at once. When you work on a real task with AI, you encounter Condition 1 because your expertise either enters the collaboration or it doesn't, and you see the difference in the output. You encounter Condition 2 because the effort of engaging deeply either happens or it doesn't, and you feel the quality shift. You encounter Condition 3 because your professional identity is either threatened or clarified by the work. You encounter Condition 4 because AI either performs as you expected or it doesn't, and your model updates. A training program addresses one condition at a time, if it addresses any. An experience addresses all four at once. That's why the system hypothesis from Chapter 8 predicts experience-first should work: if the conditions operate as a system, real tasks activate the system naturally.

One more thing from the BCG study worth sitting with. Two viable patterns emerged, centaurs and cyborgs, and neither was taught. Different people found different productive relationships with the same tool. Organizations don't need one collaboration model. They need conditions under which productive models can emerge. Mandating one pattern is the training-first mistake applied to collaboration design.

*

The executive from the opening of this chapter is looking at his slide deck differently now.

His organization didn't fail at AI adoption. It succeeded. Eighty-two percent weekly usage, 91 percent training completion, satisfaction at 4.1. By every measure the industry tracks, the implementation worked. The problem is that the industry tracks the wrong measures. Adoption metrics tell you whether people picked up the tool. They tell you nothing about what happens when they use it.

The collaboration quality gap doesn't close through mandates, training, or better tools. It closes through infrastructure: the organizational conditions that make the four psychological shifts possible.

Psychological safety, so people can engage with AI openly without social punishment. Structured experience, so people encounter the conditions through doing rather than hearing about them. And leaders who model the conditions personally, who use AI visibly, make mistakes with it publicly, and demonstrate what it looks like to bring real expertise into the collaboration rather than accepting whatever the tool produces. When a leader shares a piece of AI-assisted work and says "the tool's first draft missed the competitive dynamics entirely, so I pushed back and rebuilt that section with what I know about this market," that leader is modeling Conditions 1, 2, and 4 at once. The team doesn't need a lecture on the conditions. They need to see someone practice them and get better results because of it.

Most of this isn't new. Edmondson published on psychological safety in 1999. Experiential learning theory goes back to Kolb in the 1980s, Dewey long before that. The leadership modeling principle is as old as organizational psychology itself. The underlying insights are established. The AI-specific application is the contribution. And the application matters, because by the surveys' account the problem isn't easing: 79 percent of organizations reporting challenges in 2026, and the reported number rose year over year. The companies spending the most on AI tools are often the furthest from productive collaboration, because they've invested in everything except the conditions that determine whether the investment produces value.

An organization can't mandate its people into productive AI collaboration, any more than a therapist can order a client into insight. What it can build is the infrastructure: safety, structured experience, visible modeling. The conditions under which the four psychological shifts happen naturally, through the work itself. No workshop required. No certification needed. Just an environment where bringing your genuine expertise to AI collaboration is safe, visible, and valued.

That's the organizational argument, and it is a set of conditions rather than a playbook, a governance framework, or another change management methodology with a four-letter acronym: the same conditions the book has been describing since Chapter 5, applied to the environment that either makes them possible or quietly destroys them.

Most of your people are using AI already. The question for any leader is whether they're bringing themselves to the collaboration, and the organization you've built has more to do with the answer than the tools you've bought.

Notes

1. Writer, "Enterprise AI Adoption Report" (2026). Survey: 79% of organizations report AI adoption challenges; 54% of C-suite respondents agree AI adoption is "tearing their company apart." Survey language; dated snapshot.
2. BCG, "AI Adoption Puzzle: Why Usage Is Up but Impact Is Not" (2025).
3. BCG, "AI at Work 2025: Momentum Builds, but Gaps Remain" (June 2025). Third annual global AI at Work survey. 85% of leaders regularly use AI; 51% of frontline employees.
4. Klarna. See Chapter 4, Note 16, for the sourced record (February 2024 announcement; May 2025 Bloomberg interview).
5. Wu, S., Liu, Y., Ruan, M., Chen, S., & Xie, X.-Y. (2025). "Human-generative AI collaboration enhances task performance but undermines human's intrinsic motivation." *Scientific Reports*, 15, 15105. DOI: 10.1038/s41598-025-98385-2. See Chapter 5, Note 4.

6. Deci, E.L. & Ryan, R.M. (1985). *Intrinsic Motivation and Self-Determination in Human Behavior.* Plenum Press. Ryan, R.M. & Deci, E.L. (2000). "Self-determination theory and the facilitation of intrinsic motivation, social development, and well-being." *American Psychologist,* 55(1), 68-78.

7. Reif, J.A., Larrick, R.P., & Soll, J.B. (2025). "Evidence of a social evaluation penalty for using AI." *Proceedings of the National Academy of Sciences,* 122(19), e2426766122. DOI: 10.1073/pnas.2426766122. Four preregistered experiments, N = 4,439. 9% competence penalty overall; 13% for female engineers; 26% for female engineers evaluated by male non-adopters.

8. Edmondson, A.C. (1999). "Psychological safety and learning behavior in work teams." *Administrative Science Quarterly,* 44(2), 350-383. See also: Edmondson, A.C. (2018). *The Fearless Organization: Creating Psychological Safety in the Workplace for Learning, Innovation, and Growth.* Wiley.

9. Google re:Work, "Guide: Understand team effectiveness" (Project Aristotle), 2015–2016. Study of 180 Google teams; psychological safety identified as the leading factor in team effectiveness.

10. Dell'Acqua, F., McFowland, E. III, Mollick, E., Lifshitz-Assaf, H., Kellogg, K.C., Rajendran, S., Krayer, L., Candelon, F., & Lakhani, K.R. (2026). "Navigating the jagged technological frontier." *Organization Science.* DOI: 10.1287/orsc.2025.21838. See Chapter 8, Note 5 for figures.

11. Thomann, H. & Deutscher, V. (2025). "Scaffolding through prompts in digital learning: A systematic review and meta-analysis of effectiveness on learning achievement." *Educational Research Review,* 47, 100686. DOI: 10.1016/j.edurev.2025.100686. 68 studies; d = 0.394 (adjusted d = 0.220).

12. Kirschner, P.A., Sweller, J., & Clark, R.E. (2006). "Why minimal guidance during instruction does not work: An analysis of the failure of constructivist, discovery, problem-based, experiential, and inquiry-based teaching." *Educational Psychologist,* 41(2), 75-86. DOI: 10.1207/s15326985ep4102_1.

13. Bastani, H., et al. (2025). "Generative AI without guardrails can harm learning." *Proceedings of the National Academy of Sciences,* 122(26), e2422633122. See Chapter 1, Note 12.

14. Kolb, D.A. (1984). *Experiential Learning: Experience as the Source of Learning and Development.* Prentice-Hall.

CHAPTER 11

The Invitation

A therapist waits for a specific moment. Not the moment when the client understands the problem: understanding comes early, sometimes in the first session. Not the moment when the client describes the solution, either. People can articulate what they should do long before they can do it. The moment the therapist waits for is different. It's the moment the client sees themselves clearly enough that the next step becomes obvious without being named.

It doesn't look like a breakthrough. There's no dramatic confession, no cathartic release. It usually looks like a pause. A sentence that trails off mid-thought. A reconsideration of something the client said twenty minutes ago, or three sessions ago, that didn't land then but lands now. The client's face changes, not to relief, exactly, but to recognition. They've been looking at something without seeing it, and now they see it.

The therapist didn't put the insight there. That's the part most people misunderstand about therapy. The therapist created the conditions: safety enough to be honest, structure enough to stay focused, challenge enough to keep the client from settling into comfortable stories about themselves. The insight was the client's. It always is. The therapist couldn't have generated it. Only the client has access to the raw material of their own experience, their own patterns, their own reasons for doing what they do. What the therapist provides is the environment in which that raw material becomes visible.

This book has been creating those conditions.

*

For ten chapters, you've been looking at a pattern. You saw it first in a conference room: a founder who spent forty thousand dollars on a CRM nobody used, not because the software was bad but because using it meant seeing something about his team he wasn't ready to see. You saw the same pattern in the research: 106 experiments finding that human-AI collaboration, on average, produced less than the best of either human or AI alone, with the losses concentrated in decision tasks and the gains in creation work where the human brought real expertise. Developers in early 2025, 19 percent slower while believing they were 20 percent faster. A thousand students whose AI-boosted performance cratered the moment the tool was taken away.

You watched the conventional responses fail. Training that increased knowledge without changing behavior. Prompting techniques that expired with every model update. Change management playbooks that addressed every dimension of the problem except the one that mattered: identity. A multibillion-dollar training industry aimed at the wrong layer.

Then you looked underneath the surface and found where the problem actually lives: the mental model. The set of assumptions about who you are in the collaboration and what your role is when you sit down with a tool that can do parts of your job. You learned a name for the variable that governs the coupling: how much of your capability enters the collaboration, and how much of the tool's you draw out. You learned that the relationship between human capability and AI capability is multiplicative, which means a low multiplier doesn't just reduce value. It collapses it. And you learned four conditions that move the multiplier toward a place where the collaboration actually works.

You are the scarce input. The collaboration demands more of you, not less. Your professional identity is clarified, not threatened. Calibration is a continuous practice.

None of that was information you lacked before you opened this book. The founder with the CRM didn't lack information about how CRMs work. The developers in the METR study didn't lack coding skill. The students in the Wharton experiment didn't lack intelligence. What they lacked was a way of seeing the collaboration that made their own contribution feel both essential and possible.

That's what the four conditions provide. Not knowledge. Not technique. A way of seeing.

*

The scale of the opportunity is staggering, once you know what you're looking at.

Microsoft has roughly 450 million commercial users on its 365 platform, and as of early 2026 a small slice of them, a few percent by the January disclosures and more by April, had adopted the paid AI assistant already wired into their workday. The rest had it at hand and left it there. And of the people who did try it and quit, Chapter 8 told you what nearly half of them said: they couldn't tell when to trust it. They understood the tool well enough; what it never earned was trust through reliable collaboration.

Those are numbers about a relationship problem. The tool is there. The infrastructure is deployed. Hundreds of millions of people have access to a collaborator with extraordinary processing power, broad knowledge, and unlimited patience. What's missing is the connection: the psychological bridge between the human and the tool that turns access into value.

Think about what even a modest improvement means. Picture someone near the low end of the range Chapter 4 described, bringing a fraction of what they know and accepting what comes back. Now picture the same person bringing most of it. The tool didn't get better. The person didn't get smarter. The relationship changed, and what comes out of it is a different kind of work, the kind only that person could have produced.

Now multiply that across an organization. Across an industry. Across the hundreds of millions of people with the tool already on their desktops.

The gap that Chapter 1 described looks different from this side of the book. It's still real. It's still enormous. But it's not a failure to analyze. It's a surface to work on. Every person who starts bringing what they know into the collaboration is a categorical change in output with zero additional technology investment. The return isn't in the next model upgrade. It's in the next mental model upgrade. And unlike model upgrades, which require billions of dollars and the resources of the largest technology companies on earth, a mental model upgrade requires something far simpler and far harder: a shift in how one person sees their relationship to one tool. Simpler because it costs nothing. Harder because it asks you to change how you see yourself.

Every generation has a version of the "technology is unprecedented" claim, and every generation overstates it. So here is the narrower claim, the one this book can stand behind. This is the first time this many knowledge workers have had a fluent collaborator on the desk, and the first time we've had a way to think about the collaboration-quality layer, the during-use space where the value is created or destroyed, that is specific enough to act on. The four conditions are structural, and they apply to every collaboration, with every tool, across every domain where human judgment matters.

*

Here's the reframe that matters most.

When organizations look at their AI adoption numbers and see mediocre results, the default interpretation is that their people are deficient. They lack skills. They lack motivation. They lack the willingness to change. The interventions follow the diagnosis: more training, more incentives, more mandates. And when the mandates produce the same pattern Chapter 1 documented (usage up, impact flat), the conclusion is that the people need even more training, even stronger incentives, even clearer mandates.

The cycle is familiar to anyone who's watched organizational change efforts fail. It's also familiar to anyone who's been in therapy.

A client who keeps returning to the same self-destructive pattern isn't failing because they lack information about what they should do. They know what they should do. They can describe it in detail. They've read the books, done the exercises, listened to the podcasts. The knowledge is there. What's missing is the internal shift that makes the knowledge actionable: a change in how they see themselves and their situation that turns "I know I should" into "I can see why I do, and I can see what's different now."

The same dynamic operates at organizational scale with AI. The people aren't deficient. They're unsupported. Nobody has given them a productive way to think about their relationship to the tool they're being asked to use. They've been given instructions: use AI. They've been given training: here's how AI works. They've been given deadlines: by Q3, everyone should be using it. What they haven't been given is the psychological infrastructure that makes productive collaboration possible.

The distinction matters because it changes what you do about it. If the problem is deficiency, you train harder and mandate faster. If the problem is support, you build something different: conditions under which people can discover their own productive relationship with AI. An environment in which the shift can happen, rather than a playbook to follow or a set of rules to memorize.

The difference between a mandate and a condition is the difference every therapist understands. You can tell a client to change their behavior. You can explain why the change would be good for them. You can show them data proving that their current behavior isn't working. They will sit in the chair, agree with every word, and walk out and do exactly what they were doing before. They aren't resistant, and they aren't stupid. The instruction reached their understanding without touching their mental model. The knowing changed. The seeing didn't.

The director of strategy from Chapter 2 is the case in point. Three AI certification programs. She can explain transformer architecture in a meeting and debate training data ethics at a conference. She uses AI daily. Her deliverables haven't improved, because nothing in her extensive education about AI has touched the mental model that governs how she actually works with it. She still types a request and accepts what comes back. She still leaves her eight years of industry-specific pattern recognition outside the collaboration. She's not deficient. She's the training industry's best-case scenario, and the best case still isn't working. Another certification won't change it. She needs a different way of seeing her role in the collaboration. Not "learn more about the tool" but "bring more of yourself to the work."

Behavior change that sticks doesn't come from instruction. It comes from a shift in how someone sees themselves and their situation. A shift that, once it happens, makes the old behavior feel wrong from the inside rather than wrong because someone told you so.

*

That's why this book hasn't given you a playbook.

A playbook is a set of instructions. Instructions reach understanding. What the four conditions aim for is different: a change in how you see the collaboration itself. When you internalize that you are the scarce input, you stop waiting for AI to produce the answer and start bringing the judgment that makes any answer worth having. When you accept that the collaboration demands more of you, you stop measuring success by how easy the tool feels and start measuring it by how much of your thinking entered the output. When your professional identity is clarified rather than threatened, you stop defending the parts of your expertise that AI can replicate and start leaning into the parts it can't. When calibration becomes a practice rather than an anxiety, you develop the steady habit of checking whether your mental model still fits the tool's actual capabilities.

None of these are things someone can do for you. That's the point. And it's also why the conventional interventions keep failing. Training delivers knowledge, but knowing you're the scarce input is not the same as feeling it in the moment when AI produces something faster and more polished than you could have written alone. Change management delivers process, but no process can address the identity question that surfaces when a tool does the thing you've built your career around doing. Prompting workshops deliver technique, but technique without a mental model that values your own contribution just produces more efficient surrender.

The four conditions work at the layer where these interventions don't reach. They don't teach you about AI. They change how you see yourself in relation to AI. And that change, once it happens, is more durable than training. You don't need to re-learn that you're the scarce input every quarter. You don't need a refresher course on identity clarification. Once the lens is in place, it tends to stay, and the fourth condition is there for when it drifts, because calibration is built into the framework as a continuous practice rather than a one-time achievement.

What does the shift look like when it starts to happen? It's quieter than you'd expect. It's a financial analyst who stops accepting AI's first draft of a risk assessment and instead feeds in her own hypothesis about what's driving the anomaly she noticed in last quarter's data. She was already doing this kind of analysis before AI; the tool didn't create the expertise. But the mental model shift changed what she brought to the collaboration. Before, she was asking AI to do the analysis. Now she's using AI to pressure-test her own thinking. Same tool. Same subscription. Different relationship.

It's the product manager from Chapter 8, on the Monday-shaped day rather than the Friday-shaped one, catching herself about to accept a competitive analysis that reads well and adding the one thing she knows that isn't in any dataset. The effort of adding her own judgment felt like extra work. It was the multiplier in action.

It's an engineering lead who stops treating AI code suggestions as answers and starts treating them as first drafts that need her architectural judgment, not because she distrusts the tool, but because she understands that the tool doesn't know the technical debt buried in the module it's suggesting she refactor. She's not fighting the tool. She's not surrendering to it. She's collaborating with it, and the collaboration demands more of her than either fighting or surrendering ever did.

These aren't dramatic transformations. They're adjustments in posture: small shifts in what someone brings to the collaboration and how they hold their own judgment in relation to the tool's output. But the cumulative effect is enormous, because each shift moves the multiplier, and the multiplier touches everything.

*

The word "conditions" is deliberate, and it connects to something I've been circling since the Introduction.

In therapy, a therapist doesn't install insight into a client. Insight isn't a package you can deliver. What a therapist does is create conditions: psychological safety, focused attention, honest reflection, and enough challenge to keep the client from settling into comfortable stories about themselves. Under those conditions, the client's own capacity for self-understanding does the work. The therapist structures the environment. The client does the seeing.

Carl Rogers described the core facilitative conditions in 1957: unconditional positive regard, empathy, and congruence. The intervention isn't the therapist's expertise applied to the client's problem. The intervention is the relationship itself, structured so that the client can access their own resources. The therapist who tries to fix the client directly, who prescribes solutions and delivers instructions, produces compliance at best. The therapist who creates conditions for self-correction produces change that lasts because the client owns it.

The four conditions of H(x)AI follow the same structural logic. They don't tell you how to use AI. They create the psychological environment in which productive collaboration becomes possible. Condition 1 provides the self-efficacy foundation: if you don't believe your contribution matters, you won't contribute, regardless of how many workshops you attend. Condition 2 provides the engagement structure: if the effort feels unnecessary, you'll coast, and the output will show it. Condition 3 provides the safety: if the tool threatens who you believe you are, you'll either surrender your judgment or fight the tool on every point, and both responses waste the collaboration. Condition 4 provides the reality-testing mechanism: without it, even a productive mental model drifts out of alignment as AI capabilities change underneath you.

Together, they form a self-correcting system. Not a checklist you complete and move on from. A set of conditions you maintain, the way a therapist maintains a therapeutic relationship session after session. The conditions don't fix anything. They make it possible for you to see the collaboration clearly enough that the right action becomes obvious.

This is why the metaphor that opened the Introduction is the structural logic of the entire framework, and was never only a metaphor. The organizational therapist watching the CRM founder blame the software while the real problem sat between him and the tool was seeing what this book teaches you to see: the layer where the relationship lives, where the mental model operates, where value is created or destroyed. The four conditions are the therapeutic structure that makes that layer visible and workable.

I keep returning to this: the most important thing a therapist does is not the thing most people think a therapist does. Most people think therapy is about the therapist's expertise, their ability to diagnose what's wrong and prescribe what to fix. But decades of psychotherapy outcome research, synthesized in Wampold and Imel's analysis of what makes therapy work, tell a different story. The strongest predictor of successful therapy isn't the therapist's technique or theoretical orientation. It's the quality of the therapeutic relationship: whether the conditions exist for the client to do their own work. The expertise matters. The conditions matter more.

The same is true here. AI expertise matters. Understanding the tools, knowing their capabilities and limits, developing skill in working with them: all of that matters. But the conditions matter more. On judgment work, a person with modest AI skills and a productive mental model will usually outperform a person with deep AI expertise and a collapsed multiplier. Because the person with the productive mental model brings something into the collaboration that no amount of technical skill can substitute for: their own judgment, applied with confidence, checked with honesty, and directed by a clear understanding of what they contribute that the tool cannot.

*

The founder in the Introduction never did open that CRM.

I don't know what happened to him. Maybe he found a different tool that required less transparency. Maybe he sold the agency and the problem became someone else's. Maybe he's still telling himself the software was clunky. What I know is that his failure wasn't about the CRM. It was about a mental model that couldn't accommodate what the tool required of him: transparency about how his team actually worked, honesty about the gaps between what they promised and what they delivered. The tool asked him to see his team clearly. He chose to see the tool as the problem instead.

I should be honest about what this framework doesn't do.

Not every job has a judgment layer underneath the mechanical. For some work, AI represents genuine displacement, and pretending that identity clarification will solve that is dishonest. A data entry specialist whose job is entirely mechanical can't "find the judgment underneath" because the job was defined by the mechanical work. The four conditions are addressed to people whose work contains genuine expertise, contextual knowledge, and professional judgment that AI cannot replicate. That's a large number of people. It's not everyone. Acknowledging the difference is part of the honesty this book owes its reader.

For those whose work does contain that layer, the conditions change the equation. But even there, the change isn't automatic and it isn't easy. The founder with the CRM didn't lack the capacity to see his team clearly. He lacked the willingness. The conditions create the possibility of the shift. They don't guarantee it. Some people will read this book, recognize the pattern, and change how they work with AI starting tomorrow. Some will recognize the pattern and find that the identity question is harder than they expected: letting go of the mechanical parts of their expertise, the parts that felt most solid because they were most measurable, requires a kind of professional courage that no framework can install.

That's fine. The conditions are a practice, not a conversion experience. You don't have to arrive at the perfect mental model on your first attempt. You have to start noticing: what am I bringing to this? What am I withholding? Where am I coasting? Where am I fighting? The noticing is the practice. The conditions give it structure, and Chapter 9 gave it a Tuesday.

That choice is available to you, too. After everything this book has laid out, you can close it and return to whatever relationship you currently have with AI. Type a request, accept what comes back. Or reject AI entirely, insist your expertise doesn't need augmentation, defend the mechanical parts of your work as though they were the essential ones. Both options remain open. Both will feel rational from the inside, just as they felt rational to the surrenderers and the fighters this book has been describing since page one.

But you can also choose something harder and more honest. You can look at the next AI interaction you have and ask a different set of questions. Not "what should I prompt?" but "what am I bringing to this that the tool can't generate on its own?" Not "is this output good enough?" but "did I bring enough of my own judgment to make this output genuinely mine?" Not "does AI threaten my job?" but "what does AI reveal about where my real value lies?"

Those questions don't have final answers. That's the calibration part. The answers shift as the tools change, as your expertise develops, as new capabilities emerge and old assumptions stop fitting. The conditions aren't a destination you reach. They're a practice you maintain. The way a therapist holds the space session after session, you hold the conditions collaboration after collaboration. Some days you'll bring everything you have and the output will reflect it. Some days you'll catch yourself coasting and need to pull yourself back. Some days you'll discover that the tool has gotten better at something you thought only you could do, and you'll need to find the next layer of judgment that's yours alone. That's not failure. That's the practice working.

*

The problem was the mental model all along: the set of assumptions about who you are in the collaboration when you sit down with a machine that can do parts of your job. The tool, the knowledge, the technique, and the willingness to change were all present in the rooms where it failed.

The framework this book offers doesn't fix that problem. A framework doesn't fix anything, the same way a therapist doesn't fix a client. What it does is change how you see. And once you see the collaboration differently, once you recognize yourself as the essential contributor rather than the operator, once you accept that the effort of genuine engagement is the multiplier rather than the obstacle, once your identity is clarified rather than threatened, once calibration becomes a practice you maintain rather than a worry you suppress, the behavior changes. Not because someone instructed you. Because you can see what to do.

That's the therapist's insight, applied at the scale this moment requires. You don't fix people. You create the conditions under which they can see clearly enough to fix themselves.

The client across the table — the one the therapist has been waiting for — doesn't need to be told what to do next. The insight is already theirs. The conditions made it visible, and now it's obvious in the way that real insights always are: not because someone explained it, but because the person finally saw what was already there.

The four conditions are in front of you now. What you do with them is yours.

Notes

1. Microsoft earnings disclosures, FY2026 Q2 (January 28, 2026: ~15 million paid Microsoft 365 Copilot seats against a ~450-million commercial base) and FY2026 Q3 (April 29, 2026: "over 20 million" paid seats). Recon Analytics survey data (2025): 44% of lapsed users cited distrust of answers. Dated snapshots; see Chapter 1, Note 20 and Chapter 8, Note 1.
2. Vaccaro, M., Almaatouq, A., & Malone, T. (2024). "When combinations of humans and AI are useful: A systematic review and meta-analysis." *Nature Human Behaviour*, 8(12), 2293-2303. DOI: 10.1038/s41562-024-02024-1. See Chapter 1, Note 1.
3. Becker, J., Rush, N., Barnes, B., & Rein, D. (2025). "Measuring the impact of early-2025 AI on experienced open-source developer productivity." METR. arXiv:2507.09089. See also Becker et al. (2026), METR, February 24, 2026. See Chapter 1, Notes 6–7.
4. Bastani, H., Bastani, O., Sungu, A., Ge, H., Kabakcı, Ö., & Mariman, R. (2025). "Generative AI without guardrails can harm learning: Evidence from high school mathematics." *Proceedings of the National Academy of Sciences*, 122(26), e2422633122. See Chapter 1, Note 12.
5. Rogers, C.R. (1957). "The necessary and sufficient conditions of therapeutic personality change." *Journal of Consulting Psychology*, 21(2), 95-102. Describes the core facilitative conditions for therapeutic change: unconditional positive regard, empathy, and congruence.
6. Wampold, B.E. & Imel, Z.E. (2015). *The Great Psychotherapy Debate: The Evidence for What Makes Psychotherapy Work* (2nd ed.). Routledge. Synthesizes the common-factors evidence: the quality of the therapeutic

relationship predicts outcomes more strongly than technique or theoretical orientation.

The Companion

The four conditions are a practice, and a practice needs a place. AIRAA is that place: the interactive companion to this book, built on the same H(x)AI model. Learn the frame. Notice your patterns. Practice the four conditions against your actual working week. It's free, with an email sign-in and no password.

airaa.org/empowered

The book gave you the lens. The companion is where you point it at your own work.

Acknowledgments

For all the friends and family who let me babble for over two years: I'm sorry, and thank you. Having no idea what I'm talking about but believing in me anyway is truly a special form of love.

To the people who influenced this book:

Matt Griffith, for relentless advocacy.

Doug Karr, for brilliance and enthusiasm.

Jon Arnold, for giving me the courage to be an asshole to AI.

Matt Nettleton, for being a stonewall to bounce bad ideas off.

Daniel Fuller, for being the first to affirm the problem.

Jason Beutler, for time and generosity.

John Qualls, for finding it "very interesting."

Bibliography

*

Academic and Research Sources

Bainbridge, L. (1983). "Ironies of automation." *Automatica*, 19(6), 775-779.

Bandura, A. (1977). "Self-efficacy: Toward a unifying theory of behavioral change." *Psychological Review*, 84(2), 191-215.

Barcaui, A. (2025). "ChatGPT as a cognitive crutch: Evidence from a randomized controlled trial on knowledge retention." *Social Sciences & Humanities Open*, 12, 102287. DOI: 10.1016/j.ssaho.2025.102287.

Bastani, H., Bastani, O., Sungu, A., Ge, H., Kabakci, O., & Mariman, R. (2025). "Generative AI without guardrails can harm learning: Evidence from high school mathematics." *Proceedings of the National Academy of Sciences*, 122(26), e2422633122. DOI: 10.1073/pnas.2422633122.

Becker, J., Rush, N., Barnes, B., & Rein, D. (2025). "Measuring the impact of early-2025 AI on experienced open-source developer productivity." METR, July 10, 2025. arXiv:2507.09089.

Bjork, R.A. (1994). "Memory and metamemory considerations in the training of human beings." In J. Metcalfe & A. Shimamura (Eds.), *Metacognition: Knowing about Knowing* (pp. 185-205). MIT Press.

Brehm, J.W. (1966). *A Theory of Psychological Reactance*. Academic Press.

Brod, C. (1984). *Technostress: The Human Cost of the Computer Revolution*. Addison-Wesley.

Brynjolfsson, E., Li, D., & Raymond, L. (2023). "Generative AI at Work." NBER Working Paper No. 31161. Formally published in *The Quarterly Journal of Economics* (2025).

Buçinca, Z., Malaya, M.B., & Gajos, K.Z. (2021). "To trust or to think: Cognitive forcing functions can reduce overreliance on AI in AI-assisted decision-making." *Proceedings of the ACM on Human-Computer Interaction*, 5(CSCW1), Article 188. DOI: 10.1145/3449287.

Cymek, D.H., Truckenbrodt, A., & Onnasch, L. (2023). "Lean back or lean in? Exploring social loafing in human-robot teams." *Frontiers in Robotics and AI*, 10, 1249252. DOI: 10.3389/frobt.2023.1249252.

Davis, F.D. (1989). "Perceived usefulness, perceived ease of use, and user acceptance of information technology." *MIS Quarterly*, 13(3), 319-340.

Deci, E.L. & Ryan, R.M. (1985). *Intrinsic Motivation and Self-Determination in Human Behavior*. Plenum Press. See also: Ryan, R.M. & Deci, E.L. (2000). "Self-Determination Theory and the facilitation of intrinsic motivation, social development, and well-being." *American Psychologist*, 55(1), 68-78.

Dell'Acqua, F., McFowland, E. III, Mollick, E., Lifshitz-Assaf, H., Kellogg, K.C., Rajendran, S., Krayer, L., Candelon, F., & Lakhani, K.R. (2026). "Navigating the Jagged Technological Frontier: Field Experimental Evidence of the Effects of Artificial Intelligence on Knowledge Worker Productivity and Quality." *Organization Science* (March 2026). DOI: 10.1287/orsc.2025.21838. Originally Harvard Business School Working Paper No. 24-013 (September 2023).

Edmondson, A.C. (1999). "Psychological safety and learning behavior in work teams." *Administrative Science Quarterly*, 44(2), 350-383. See also: Edmondson, A.C. (2018). *The Fearless Organization: Creating Psychological Safety in the Workplace for Learning, Innovation, and Growth*. Wiley.

Everett, S.S., Bunning, B.J., Jain, P., Lopez, I., Agarwal, A., Desai, M., Gallo, R., Goh, E., Kadiyala, V.B., Kanjee, Z., Koshy, J.M., Olson, A., Rodman, A., Schulman, K., Strong, E., Chen, J.H., & Horvitz, E. (2026). "From tool to teammate in a randomized controlled trial of clinician-AI collaborative workflows for diagnosis." *npj Digital Medicine*, 9, 409. DOI: 10.1038/s41746-026-02545-1.

Fernandes, D., Villa, S., Nicholls, S., Haavisto, O., Buschek, D., Schmidt, A., Kosch, T., Shen, C., & Welsch, R. (2025). "AI makes you smarter but none the wiser: The disconnect between performance and metacognition." *Computers in Human Behavior*, 175, 108779. DOI: 10.1016/j.chb.2025.108779.

Gentner, D. & Stevens, A.L. (Eds.) (1983). *Mental Models*. Lawrence Erlbaum Associates.

Gerlich, M. (2025). "From Offloading to Engagement: An Experimental Study on Structured Prompting and Critical Reasoning with Generative AI." *Data* (MDPI), 10(11), 172. DOI: 10.3390/data10110172.

Hemmer, P., Schemmer, M., Kuhl, N., Vossing, M., & Satzger, G. (2025). "Complementarity in human-AI collaboration: concept, sources, and evidence." *European Journal of Information Systems*, 34(6), 979-1002. DOI: 10.1080/0960085X.2025.2475962.

Hermann, E., Puntoni, S., & Morewedge, C.K. (2025). "GenAI and the psychology of work." *Trends in Cognitive Sciences*, 29(9). DOI: 10.1016/j.tics.2025.04.009.

Ibarra, H. (2003). *Working Identity: Unconventional Strategies for Reinventing Your Career*. Harvard Business School Press.

Johnson-Laird, P.N. (1983). *Mental Models: Towards a Cognitive Science of Language, Inference, and Consciousness*. Harvard University Press.

Kahneman, D. & Tversky, A. (1979). "Intuitive prediction: Biases and corrective procedures." *TIMS Studies in Management Science*, 12, 313-327.

Kirschner, P.A., Sweller, J., & Clark, R.E. (2006). "Why minimal guidance during instruction does not work: An analysis of the failure of constructivist, discovery, problem-based, experiential, and inquiry-based teaching." *Educational Psychologist*, 41(2), 75-86. DOI: 10.1207/s15326985ep4102_1.

Kolb, D.A. (1984). *Experiential Learning: Experience as the Source of Learning and Development*. Prentice-Hall.

Kruger, J. & Dunning, D. (1999). "Unskilled and unaware of it: How difficulties in recognizing one's own incompetence lead to inflated self-assessments." *Journal of Personality and Social Psychology*, 77(6), 1121-1134.

Lee, D., Pruitt, J., Zhou, T., Du, J., & Odegaard, B. (2025). "Metacognitive sensitivity: The key to calibrating trust and optimal decision making with AI." *PNAS Nexus*, 4(5), pgaf133. DOI: 10.1093/pnasnexus/pgaf133.

Lewin, K. (1936). *Principles of Topological Psychology*. McGraw-Hill.

Li, J., & Huang, J.S. (2020). "Dimensions of artificial intelligence anxiety based on integrated fear acquisition theory." *Technology in Society*, 63, 101410. DOI: 10.1016/j.techsoc.2020.101410.

Li, J., Yang, Y., Zhang, R., Liao, Q.V., Song, T., Xu, Z., & Lee, Y. (2024). "Understanding the Effects of Miscalibrated AI Confidence on User Trust, Reliance, and Decision Efficacy." *CHI 2024*. arXiv:2402.07632.

Mirbabaie, M., Brunker, F., Mollmann Frick, N.R.J., & Stieglitz, S. (2022). "The rise of artificial intelligence – understanding the AI identity threat at the workplace." *Electronic Markets*, 32(1), 73-99. DOI: 10.1007/s12525-021-00496-x.

Parasuraman, A. (2000). "Technology Readiness Index (TRI): A multiple-item scale to measure readiness to embrace new technologies." *Journal of Service Research*, 2(4), 307-320. DOI: 10.1177/109467050024001.

Parasuraman, R. & Riley, V. (1997). "Humans and automation: Use, misuse, disuse, abuse." *Human Factors*, 39(2), 230-253.

Parasuraman, R. & Wickens, C.D. (2008). "Humans: Still vital after all these years of automation." *Human Factors*, 50(3), 511-520.

Peng, S., Kalliamvakou, E., Cihon, P., & Demirer, M. (2023). "The Impact of AI on Developer Productivity: Evidence from GitHub Copilot." arXiv:2302.06590.

Reif, J.A., Larrick, R.P., & Soll, J.B. (2025). "Evidence of a social evaluation penalty for using AI." *Proceedings of the National Academy of Sciences*, 122(19). DOI: 10.1073/pnas.2426766122.

Rogers, C.R. (1957). "The necessary and sufficient conditions of therapeutic personality change." *Journal of Consulting Psychology*, 21(2), 95-102.

Romeo, G. & Conti, D. (2025). "Exploring automation bias in human-AI collaboration: a review and implications for explainable AI." *AI & Society*. DOI: 10.1007/s00146-025-02422-7.

Sahni, R. & Chilton, L.B. (2025). "Beyond AI Training: How Social and Experiential Learning Shape AI Adoption in the Workplace." Columbia University. arXiv:2502.13281. https://arxiv.org/abs/2502.13281.

Senge, P. (1990). *The Fifth Discipline: The Art and Practice of the Learning Organization*. Doubleday.

Shata, A. (2025). "'Opting out of AI': Exploring Perceptions, Reasons, and Concerns Behind Faculty Resistance to Generative AI." *Frontiers in Communication*, 10, 1614804. DOI: 10.3389/fcomm.2025.1614804.

Shonhe, L. & Min, J. (2025). "Mitigating AI-induced professional identity threat and fostering adoption in the workplace." *AI & Society*, 40, 4079-4092. DOI: 10.1007/s00146-024-02170-0.

Thomann, H. & Deutscher, V. (2025). "Scaffolding through prompts in digital learning: A systematic review and meta-analysis of effectiveness on learning achievement." *Educational Research Review*, 47, 100686. DOI: 10.1016/j.edurev.2025.100686.

Trist, E.L. & Bamforth, K.W. (1951). "Some social and psychological consequences of the longwall method of coal-getting." *Human Relations*, 4(1), 3-38.

Vaccaro, M., Almaatouq, A., & Malone, T. (2024). "When combinations of humans and AI are useful: A systematic review and meta-analysis." *Nature Human Behaviour*, 8(12), 2293-2303. DOI: 10.1038/s41562-024-02024-1.

Venkatesh, V., Morris, M.G., Davis, G.B., & Davis, F.D. (2003). "User acceptance of information technology: Toward a unified view." *MIS Quarterly*, 27(3), 425-478.

Vroom, V.H. (1964). *Work and Motivation*. John Wiley & Sons.

Wampold, B.E. & Imel, Z.E. (2015). *The Great Psychotherapy Debate: The Evidence for What Makes Psychotherapy Work* (2nd ed.). Routledge.

Wu, S., Liu, Y., Ruan, M., Chen, S., & Xie, X.-Y. (2025). "Human-generative AI collaboration enhances task performance but undermines human's intrinsic motivation." *Scientific Reports*, 15, 15105. DOI: 10.1038/s41598-025-98385-2.

Industry Reports and Analysis

Acar, O.A., Gai, P.J., Tu, Y., & Hou, Y. (2025). "Research: The Hidden Penalty of Using AI at Work." *Harvard Business Review*, August 2025.

BambooHR (2025). "Think You Can Spot AI? Think Again: 70% of Workers Get It Wrong." Conducted with Method Research. https://www.bamboohr.com/blog/ai-detection-confidence.

BCG (2025). "AI Adoption Puzzle: Why Usage Is Up But Impact Is Not." https://www.bcg.com/publications/2025/ai-adoption-puzzle-why-usage-up-impact-not.

BCG (June 2025). "AI at Work 2025: Momentum Builds, but Gaps Remain." Third annual global AI at Work survey. https://www.bcg.com/publications/2025/ai-at-work-momentum-builds-but-gaps-remain.

Becker, J., Rush, N., Cunningham, T., Rein, D., & Mahamud, K. (2026). "We are changing our developer productivity experiment design." METR, February 24, 2026. https://metr.org/blog/2026-02-24-uplift-update/.

Bersin, J. (2026). "New Research: How AI Transforms $400 Billion of Corporate Learning." joshbersin.com, February 2026.

CIO (2026). "Companies are spending billions to train workers for AI. Most of it will fail." cio.com.

CodeRabbit (2025). "State of AI vs Human Code Generation Report." Published December 17, 2025. Analysis of 470 open-source GitHub pull requests. coderabbit.ai.

Eatough, E., Ferrazzi, K., Smith, W., & Waters, S. (2026). "Why AI Adoption Stalls, According to Industry Data." *Harvard Business Review*, February 17, 2026. https://hbr.org/2026/02/why-ai-adoption-stalls-according-to-industry-data.

Faros AI (2025). "The AI Productivity Paradox: AI Coding Assistants Increase Developer Output, But Not Company Productivity." Published July 23, 2025. https://faros.ai/blog/ai-software-engineering.

Google re:Work (2015–2016). "Guide: Understand team effectiveness" (Project Aristotle). Study of 180 Google teams.

Li, J., Zhu, F., & Hua, P. (2025). "Overcoming the Organizational Barriers to AI Adoption." *Harvard Business Review*, November 11, 2025.

Mann, H. (2026). "AI Productivity Blind Spot." *California Management Review Insight* (Frontier section), January 26, 2026.

McKinsey (December 2025). "Redefine AI upskilling as a change imperative." [Reports findings from Sahni & Chilton (2025).]

METR (2025). "Measuring the Impact of Early-2025 AI on Experienced Open-Source Developer Productivity." Published July 10, 2025. arXiv:2507.09089.

MIT NANDA (2025). "The GenAI Divide: State of AI in Business 2025." MIT NANDA initiative, July 2025. Based on 150 leader interviews, 350-employee survey, and 300 public AI deployment analysis.

Writer (2026). Enterprise AI adoption report.

News and Case Studies

CNET AI Article Debacle. Multiple news sources, 2023. CNET published 77 AI-generated financial articles; 41 required corrections (over 50%), including basic math errors and plagiarized phrases.

Google Gemini Failures. Multiple news sources, 2024-2025. Historically inaccurate diverse image generation (February 2024), threatening messages, and self-negative coding spiral (2025).

Hallucinated Legal Citations. Multiple court records and legal reporting, 2023-2025. Approximately 712 legal decisions involving hallucinated AI content (90% occurring in 2025). *Mata v. Avianca* (2023): $5,000 sanction. *Noland v. Land of the Free*: 21 of 23 quotations fabricated.

Klarna (2024–2025). Press release, February 27, 2024 (AI assistant handling two-thirds of customer service chats, "doing the equivalent work of 700 full-time agents"); Siemiatkowski, S., interview with Bloomberg, May 8, 2025, as reported by CX Dive and Forbes ("As cost unfortunately seems to have been a too predominant evaluation factor when organizing this, what you end up having is lower quality"; humans recruited back into customer service).

Mata v. Avianca, Inc., No. 22-cv-1461 (S.D.N.Y. June 22, 2023), sanctions order. Attorneys sanctioned for filing a brief citing six nonexistent cases generated by ChatGPT.

Microsoft Copilot Enterprise Adoption. Microsoft earnings disclosures, FY2026 Q2 (January 28, 2026: approximately 15 million paid Microsoft 365 Copilot seats against a ~450-million commercial base) and FY2026 Q3 (April 29, 2026: "over 20 million" paid seats). Recon Analytics survey data (2025), as reported by Directions on Microsoft, Windows Central, and Computerworld: 44% of lapsed users cited distrust of answers; accuracy Net Promoter Score declined from -3.5 (July 2025) to -24.1 (September 2025). All figures are dated snapshots.

Moffatt v. Air Canada, British Columbia Civil Resolution Tribunal, February 2024. Airline held liable for incorrect bereavement-fare information provided by its website chatbot.

Government Sources

Gilbert, L. (2024). "One Year of i.AI: Reimagining Government through Artificial Intelligence." i.AI Blog, 16 December 2024. https://ai.gov.uk/blogs/one-year-of-iai-reimagining-government-through-artificial-intelligence/. [i.AI is the UK government's cross-government AI incubator under DSIT. Of 57 ideas tested, 22 were in incubation and 11 in development pipeline (alpha, beta, or scaling stages).]

About the Author

Aaron Douglas is a marketing strategist trained as an organizational psychologist and marriage and family therapist. Over a twenty-year career — organizational research, a marketing agency he founded, an alternative therapy facility he owned and operated — he kept meeting the same pattern: people resisting openness to being changed by experience. The context changed; the aim didn't: helping people become the best versions of themselves. This book turns that work toward AI. He runs Auspicious LLC, hosts the *AI Empowered* podcast, has always loved the em dash, and is an expert at falling. He lives in Indianapolis.

The first chapter of this book is free at aiempoweredbook.com, where you'll also find the *AI Empowered* podcast.

You can contact him at aaron@auspicious.llc.

www.ingramcontent.com/pod-product-compliance
Lightning Source LLC
LaVergne TN
LVHW022212200926
848481LV00006B/1932
9798996632404